The BOOK of Turkey Hunting

Dr. Ron McGaughey

Copyright © 2011 by Ronald McGaughey.
All rights reserved.

No part of this book may be reproduced in any form, by any means, electronic or otherwise, including photocopying, scanning, downloading, or by any data storage system, without written permission from the publisher.

Cover & Interior Design by Scribe Freelance

www.scribefreelance.com

Set in Bell MT

ISBN: 978-0-615-47072-6

Printed in the United States of America

ACKNOWLEDGEMENTS

I WOULD LIKE TO THANK ALL of my turkey hunting buddies for the memories. I mentioned the names of a number of my hunting buddies in this book, and there are many more who I did not mention. I am blessed to have you all as my friends.

I would like to thank Steven Holland, Emory Breed, Lance Vanlandingham, and Ed Loyless for reading the book and helping me to edit and improve it along the way. I want to thank Steven for his great work on the various illustrations that appear in the book. Steven is a talented artist and a turkey hunter. Besides that, he knows how I think after having been my student when he was in college many years ago and a good friend ever since. Communicating my ideas to him was easy, and he put them on paper. Steven, Ed, and my son Ray made major contributions to the editing of the book. Emory and Lance shared ideas for making it better.

I would like to thank my buddy Tim Watson for helping me become a pretty good public land turkey hunter. He is the best I know on public land! I would like also to thank David Shealy, a former student from many years ago, for helping me to understand the publication process, thus making it possible for you to have this book in front of you.

Last, but most important, I would like to thank God for making me a turkey hunter and blessing me with the opportunity to enjoy His grand creation.

Table of Contents

Chapter 1: Introduction	7
Chapter 2: Footwear and Clothing	11
Chapter 3: Vests, Decoys, Blinds, and Other Accessories	17
Chapter 4: The Turkey Gun and Related Accessories	25
Chapter 5: Turkey Calls	28
Chapter 6: A Place to Hunt	36
Chapter 7: Turkeys and Turkey Behavior	43
Chapter 8: Scouting	52
Chapter 9: Setting up on Turkeys	60
Chapter 10: Calling a Turkey	64
Chapter 11: The Classic Morning Hunt and Calling a Gobbler off the Roost	68
Chapter 12: Hunting Gobblers Throughout the Day	74
Chapter 13: Making an Effective Shot and Retrieving Your Trophy	79
Chapter 14: Using Decoys and Blinds	86
Chapter 15: Advanced Tactics for Taking Gobblers	93
Chapter 16: After the Kill	103
Chapter 17: Tips on Rio, Merriam, and Eastern Gobblers	119
Chapter 18: The Grand Sport and Turkey Hunters	128

CHAPTER 1
INTRODUCTION

I HAVE BEEN A TURKEY HUNTER FOR most of my life. I started at 12 years old, so I have been turkey hunting some 46 years. I also hunt deer, turkey, ducks, squirrels, rabbits, quail, doves, and just about anything else legal to hunt. Many of the skills that I acquired in hunting small game such as squirrels helped me to become a successful turkey hunter. My favorite sport, hands down, is turkey hunting.

When I was a small child, my Dad took me squirrel hunting a lot. We mostly still hunted, so he taught me to move silently through the woods, stopping to look and listen for periods of time, and to pay attention to every detail of my surroundings: the sights, the sounds, the smells, and the movement of critters around me. We had beagles and rabbit hunted as well. It was rabbit hunting that helped me learn to anticipate an animal's travel route and to hit a moving target. My Dad was a busy man, so we did not get to hunt as much as he would have liked, but he took me when he could.

Dad bought me a BB gun when I was about 6 or 7 years old, and thus my lifetime of hunting began in earnest. I would come home from school nearly every day, grab the BB gun, and away I would go to hunt something. My prey was primarily birds, but snakes, bullfrogs, squirrels, rabbits and other critters were not safe. I did not kill much of anything but birds until I got a pellet gun, but not for lack of trying. I learned to mimic the sounds of birds and squirrels to call them from their hiding places. I learned from Dad how to call crows into shooting range with my mouth. I made bows, arrows, and sling shots for hunting during periods when I got my BB gun put up for some infraction of my Dad's rules, like shooting a songbird. Spending time in the outdoors and with Dad helped me learn to hunt, call critters, and shoot.

Growing up in the country, and having a Dad who loved hunting, gave me the opportunity to become a hunter and woodsman. Woodsmanship is a key characteristic of a successful turkey hunter, and a deer hunter for that matter. I think most turkey and deer hunters would agree. My Dad's instruction and time spent in the woods made me a woodsman. Different people develop those skills in different ways, but they are important to one's hunting success. Hunting with people who are not woodsmen has convinced me even more that this is true.

I became interested in turkeys and turkey hunting well before I got the opportunity to hunt them. My family had land on the Bogue Chitto River outside of McComb, Mississippi. It was one of the first places in Mississippi where the Mississippi Game and Fish Department released turkeys as part of early restocking efforts. We could not hunt them for a number of years until they were well established, but those turkeys greatly aroused my curiosity. I knew one person who turkey hunted; it was the early 60s, and turkey hunting was anything but a "big" sport. That person was my Uncle Buddy. He was really a cousin, but since he was "old," I called him Uncle Buddy. He turkey hunted and was apparently pretty good at it. He would allow me to look at his turkey beards, and he showed me his old box call and a slate call, but that was about it. He certainly had no interest in teaching me anything. Uncle Buddy did accompany my Dad turkey hunting one time, but only because Dad took him to some family land that had turkeys on it out around Gillsburg, Mississippi (in Amite county, made famous by Jerry Clower). I recall Dad's excitement at seeing a turkey, but as far as I know, that is the only time Dad ever went turkey hunting. Dad's real passion was bow hunting whitetail deer.

When I was 12, my Dad got hurt and was hospitalized for a long time. I spent lots of time with my Uncle Julius during that time and for the next few summers, helping him on his farm on the Bogue Chitto River. My Uncle Norman lived right across the creek and had a wild gobbler with his domestic turkey flock. It wandered up as a jake and took up with the flock. I was fascinated with that gobbler and loved to hear him gobble. I made a call from a piece of slate I obtained by breaking a small chalk board, like the ones used by kids for drawing back then. I rounded the slate's edges off by rubbing it on concrete. When I was done, it was about 3 inches in diameter. I bored a small hole on one side with a nail. I made a striker with a piece of cedar and put a piece of corn cob on the end of it. I rounded the business end of the cedar striker off and charred it as I had seen done on my Uncle Buddy's strikers. I used a short length of baling twine to attach the striker to the slate. I used that crude call to aggravate Uncle Norman's gobbler into gobbling. I had no clue what I was doing, but if I found something that the gobbler liked, I did it. I also had the hens to listen to and that helped. Thus began my turkey calling. During the next fall hunting season, I used that crude slate call, cupped in the palm of my hand to create a sound chamber, to call up some turkeys when I was squirrel hunting. I had no camouflage back then, so they saw me and promptly departed. That was the humble beginning of a lifetime of turkey hunting.

I hunted for two years before killing a turkey, and while I hate to admit it, I first killed a hen. I had called up gobblers and scared them off several times without getting a shot, or if I shot, I missed. I had no idea at that time that a hen would come to the call, and this hen did. She saw me and jumped up to fly, catching me completely off guard. I nailed her with my Dad's old LC Smith 12 Gauge. I was proud of that shot, but disappointed when I discovered that I had killed a hen. While I wish I had a better story of my first turkey, that's it!

I hunted turkeys each spring on the Bogue Chitto through my high school years. I loved it, but was not nearly as successful a killing them as I was at scaring them off! By now, I had a Lynch World Champion Box call. I was proud of that call, and my calling was better, but I still had not really figured out how to turkey hunt. It was all trial and error—mostly error.

At Mississippi State I had a roommate named Carlton. His Dad was a turkey hunter. Carlton knew much more than me about turkey hunting, and I learned a lot from him. He taught me how to make a snuff box call (a tube call) and a diaphragm call (you could buy neither in the store back then), and he taught me how to use them. He had camouflage clothing and made me realize I needed some too! I turkey hunted some that freshman year out at Noxubee Refuge, but still without much success. I felt obligated to devote more time to the ladies, and did so for much of the rest of my college career. I remember turkey hunting only a time or two in what remained of my college years.

After college, I moved to Georgia to work for a textile company in LaGrange, Georgia. I lived in Pine Mountain for most of my years in Georgia, and in the early 80s, not sure what year, Georgia opened turkey season in my county and in surrounding counties. A gentleman from Meriwether County, Mr. Ray, had much paper company land, and a large farm leased for his various hunting clubs. I joined one of them, and became good friends with Mr. Ray. Mr. Ray allowed me to turkey hunt on the farm he had leased, but it was off limits to everyone else. That is where I started doing some serious turkey hunting. That farm was loaded with turkeys, and I killed many gobblers on it. I was older, more mature, and more dedicated to my sport at that point and determined to "get good at it." I started introducing others, like my buddies Emory, Ed, and Robert, to turkey hunting, and I have continued to do that over the years. The rest, as they say, is history. That was nearly 30 years ago. Since then, I have killed a truck load of gobblers.

In my many years of turkey hunting, I have been fortunate enough to hunt with men whom I regard as some of the best turkey hunters around. You won't see many of them in hunting videos, but you might see them in the woods before or during turkey season in Georgia, Mississippi, Arkansas, Louisiana, or Alabama. All but a few of my hunting buddies are accomplished turkey hunters. I introduced many of them, probably most of them, to turkey hunting, and some are now better at certain aspects of turkey hunting than me. Over the years, we have learned together and learned from each other. Everyone hunts a little different, calls a little different, and has different ideas about what works best. I have learned from experience, other hunters, books and articles, and seminars, and the learning never ends. I don't, nor will I ever, profess to know it all. Nearly every year a gobbler reminds me of that!

Turkey hunting is a passion with me. I have 4 college degrees—the last earned was a PhD. My college degrees prepared me for work, thus giving me a means of supporting my turkey hunting habit. I have been teaching college for the last 30 years, and instructing others in "how to do things" is my life's work. It is so much a part of me, that some of my buddies are annoyed by my "instruction" when they don't ask for it. The people who really know me would tell you that what I know best is turkey hunting and teaching. For years I have talked about writing a book on turkey hunting. I finally decided to quit talking and start writing. This book is the result.

What I aim to do with this book is tell you what I have learned over the years in becoming a turkey hunter. I will tell you what equipment is needed; some things are necessary, like a gun, and some are optional, like blinds. I will tell you how to find turkeys and a place to hunt, how to figure out gobblers (some call that patterning a bird), how to set up on turkeys, how to call turkeys, how to kill turkeys, and what to do with your turkey after the kill. I have been blessed to hunt Rio Grandes in Texas, Oklahoma, Kansas and Nebraska, Easterns in Mississippi, Georgia, Alabama, and Arkansas, and Merriams in South Dakota and Nebraska. I will share with you tactics that I have employed in taking many turkeys from all three of those subspecies. Tactics and gear requirements change somewhat when hunting different subspecies in different environments, and in different situations. I will tell you what I have learned, and hopefully it will help you be successful in hunting turkeys anywhere you may go. You will note that the Osceola is conspicuously absent. I never killed an Osceola, but I intend to give them a try before the good Lord calls me home!

What I share with you in this book can help you to get started turkey hunting and be successful at it. If you are already an accomplished turkey hunter, it will probably reaffirm much of what you know, remind you of things you may have forgotten, and it may just help you learn something new. If nothing more, the book's content should entertain you. I wrote the book for everyone interested in turkey hunting.

Last, I must warn you that turkey hunting is addictive. Each spring when turkey season ends, I experience withdrawals, and they are eased only by thinking about, talking about, and planning next year's turkey hunts. Furthermore, turkey hunting can put a strain on relationships. That is all I have to say about that!

CHAPTER 2
Footwear and Clothing

In this chapter I cover turkey hunting gear from the bottom up. I address a wide array of gear that many turkey hunters use at least some of the time. You need not have it all to start, but as time passes, and if you turkey hunt a lot, you will have much of this gear.

FOOTWEAR—BOOTS AND SOCKS

When you turkey hunt you often do a lot of walking, so you better have a comfortable pair of boots. I actually use 5 or 6 different pairs of boots because I hunt in different weather conditions and habitat. Now, don't think you have to have a different pair of boots for every place you hunt. For many years I turkey hunted in a comfortable pair of boots that I deer hunted in during the early fall. A comfortable, general purpose boot is certainly going to meet most turkey hunter's needs. In my opinion, they should not be a color that sticks out like a sore thumb, or have anything real shiny on them—turkeys have excellent vision. They should be comfortable to walk in, even for long distances, and unless you hunt the southwestern United States where there is seldom rainfall or heavy dew on the grass, they should probably be waterproof.

If you are hunting where there are lots of snakes, like swamps or the mesquite country of Texas, you need a good, comfortable pair of snake boots. I recommend they be waterproof, so you can wade through swamps, or creeks if need be. Waterproof boots will also keep your feet dry as you walk through wet fields. Knee high boots are best. Chaps may protect you from snakes and briars, but chaps tend to be noisy, hot, and cumbersome, and they won't keep your feet dry while wading through water.

If you are going to hunt mountainous terrain, you need boots that give you good ankle support and have good grip for walking and perhaps climbing on rocks. You want sure footing because you want to be able to move quickly and quietly, and you don't want to slip and fall due to lack of traction. When you try them on for size, sit down as if you were setting up on a turkey—on your butt with knees up. Do they bind your feet or ankles? They need to be comfortable to walk in, but they also need to be comfortable when you sit for long periods of time. Good turkey hunting boots should be functional and comfortable. Boots that cause discomfort when you are sitting down will cause you to reposition yourself often, and that means movement. You don't want to be moving around when you are working a turkey.

If you are hunting mostly flat terrain, roads, logging roads, fields and such, you want a good pair of walking boots that will feel good on your feet even after you have been walking for 4 or 5 miles. Something that wicks moisture away from your foot is desirable. A tennis shoe type sole can be good here as such soles have the added advantage of allowing you to feel what you are stepping on, thus helping you to avoid snapping twigs and sticks as you walk. Ankle high or 10 inch boots, preferably with GORE-TEX to make them water proof, are my preferred boots for gentle terrain.

Rubber boots are handy for hunting in places like Kansas and Nebraska where you walk through wet fields in the morning. Without waterproof boots, your feet will be wet and clammy, and that makes for discomfort later in the day. Something fairly light and waterproof that offers good traction is needed in such conditions. My buddies like the La Crosse rubber boots. I have some as well, but also wear a pair of neoprene Bogs. The Bogs are really light and offer the added advantage of warmth on crisp cool mornings. My buddies from Mississippi like the rubber boots because they often have to cross creeks while hunting, and sometimes drop down into a creek to sneak around on a turkey.

Snow is not unusual when hunting in the Dakotas or in the Rockies in the spring. If you are going to be hunting at high altitudes or in other areas where snow is possible, you need something that will keep your feet dry and warm. Here again, my neoprene Bogs fit the bill for me. They are warm, light, and waterproof. They are also camouflaged, which is the case for all my turkey hunting boots. I like to be camouflaged from head to toe when I turkey hunt. My buddies wear the same waterproof, insulated hunting boots they deer hunt in—they have an aggressive sole for good traction and good support. Good support is the only thing my Bogs lack, so I have to be rather careful when walking in them. People with weak ankles, really need something with good ankle support. A sprained or broken ankle can be a serious problem if you are in the middle of nowhere!

Don't underestimate the importance of good socks. Buy good quality socks, because if you don't, even good boots will not be as comfortable as they could be. I like socks that are made of merino wool (usually a merino wool, acrylic and spandex combination)—the more merino wool in the blend the better. These socks wick moisture away from your feet and they don't get clammy. I wear them regardless of whether it is hot or cold. I have thin, thick, and very thick socks made of merino wool. It helps when they are crafted to fit the contour of your feet, providing padding where needed without excessive bulk. Many companies make such socks, and while they are not cheap, they are worth the investment. Comfort starts with your feet. I would avoid cotton socks because, if cotton socks get wet, they get clammy and start shifting on your foot usually ending up in a wad—not very comfortable. There are good socks made from synthetic materials that are comfortable and capable of providing warmth, wicking away moisture, etc. Be sure that the socks you wear turkey hunting are comfortable for the conditions you will experience while turkey hunting. When I know I will be in the field all day, I carry a second pair of socks to change into at some point during the day—it is refreshing! By all means, try out your boot/sock combination before you take off on a long walk in them. If you don't, you might wish you had!

Boots: From left to right top to bottom are Danner Snake boots (waterproof as well), knee high rubber boots, Cabela's Sneakers (light, waterproof, and comfortable), LL Bean Hunter Hikers (200 Grams of Thinsulate for warmth, good tread for rough terrain, and comfortable), and Bogs (good for cold weather and snow—waterproof).

PANTS AND SHIRTS

Pants and shirts should be camouflage, and the pattern should reasonably well match the environment where you intend to hunt. There are many good patterns on the market today, so you can find a pattern appropriate for any environment. I like patterns with lots of brown and gray for the rugged mountains of the west (Natural Gear, Mossy Oak Break and Real Tree Hardwoods all work well), as I generally set up next to trees or rocks. Most of the trees are conifers, like pines, spruce, and cedar, and there are Aspen groves as well, so browns and grays with black and a little green blend in well. I like patterns with lots of green for hunting the croplands of Nebraska and Kansas, and for hunting the mesquite country of Texas. I like Mossy Oak Obsession in particular because it has lots of green, but also includes tree bark patterns that blend well with a tree trunk (mesquite and locusts trees are common). This pattern works well in the south when it starts to green up in spring. When hunting hardwood forests, patterns that blend in well with tree trunks and with the forest floor are good choices. Realtree Advantage or APG works well in these areas, as does Mossy Oak New Breakup and Mossy Oak Forest Floor. Other patterns like Superfladge and Natural Gear also work well.

The key is to blend in! After I wash my camo, I line dry it out in my yard right next to the woods to keep it scent free and color fast. I can observe quite easily what patterns blend in the best against the backdrop of cedar, honey suckle, and post oaks. As far as pant style, I prefer bibs, because I like the large chest pocket in the middle of most bibs. That is where I put my mouth calls. I can also stick my wingbone call in that pocket to keep it from bouncing around making noise—also protects it. I drop my binoculars inside the bibs to protect them and keep them from bouncing around. There is nothing wrong with regular pants—I wear them as well, especially when it is very hot. I like the ones with 6 pockets (cargo pockets on the legs), because they offer plenty of storage as well. Whatever style of pants you wear, make sure they are not too tight. You don't want them binding you when you sit down against a tree and draw your knees up towards you, the position I most often assume when I set up. I like pants or bibs long enough to cover down past the top of my boots, so that my socks don't show (most of my socks are not camo). There are primarily two styles of shirts, T-shirts (long sleeve or short) and button up. I like and use both. I generally wear a long sleeve T-shirt if it is very hot, and prefer something cotton or some other cool fabric (modern moisture wicking polyesters work well). I wear a button up on cooler days, and often wear the T-shirt under a button-up shirt, so I can remove the button-up as the day heats up. That is a typical day in most places I hunt in the spring—starts out cool, and then warms up. I highly recommend dressing in layers so you can add layers as needed or remove as needed to stay comfortable.

COATS, VESTS AND RAIN GEAR

Coats and vests are needed when temperatures are colder. I like something that is light, has plenty of pockets, and can be folded into a compact package and carried when need be. If I have to walk a long way into where I am going to hunt, I often carry a fleece pullover and/or a fleece vest in my turkey vest. I put them on when I start to hunt. If it is really cold and the walk in is short, I wear them on the walk in. I can carry them in my vest again after it warms up, and I have to shed them to cool off. In either case, think light weight and compact. I like fleece because it fits the bill for me. Some fleece offers the added advantage of being waterproof and most fleece garments are very warm and quiet. My fleece vest and pullover combo keeps me warm on even very cool mornings. When it is very cold, as it sometimes is in South Dakota in the spring, I use a coat that is light weight, warm, and water proof. Snow at that time of year can be heavy and wet, and a high wind when it is cold can be brutal. Be prepared with a coat that will keep you both warm and dry. I also have waterproof pants that I wear when it is snowing. The coat and pants are Mossy Oak Breakup and they blend in well, not with the snow, but with the trees and rocks I usually sit against. I have a rain suit that is compact and light as well as a couple of rain ponchos. No matter the temperature, I carry one or the other of these rain garments in my vest when it looks like rain. This simple practice has saved numerous hunts for me—kept me in the field in spite of the rain. Here too, the pattern of the garment should be appropriate for the area you intend to hunt. Blend in!

BASE LAYERS

I like wearing a base layer in anything but very warm weather. I like a mid-weight polypropylene if it is pretty cold and light weight polypropylene if it is just chilly in the mornings or evenings. This material is warm, wicks away moisture, and it is light. I can strip it off if it gets hot, and put it in my turkey vest. It dries fast as well. I have a couple pair of long johns that are layered polypropylene and merino wool. They are warm, light, and they wick moisture very well. There are numerous warm weather base layers that are comfortable. Not everyone likes them, but I do because they allow my clothes to slide freely over my body as I move—they don't bind me in any way. A warm-weather base layer is not something that is essential, but I do believe that under layers that keep you warm when it is cold are necessary. Just like deer hunting, if you sit for a while and get cold, you will have trouble sitting still and concentrating on your hunting. In the rugged mountains of the west, or secluded areas anywhere, inadequate clothing is not just uncomfortable, it's dangerous!

GLOVES

I consider gloves to be essential gear. While you can use camo paint to camouflage your hands, it is a bit messy. I did that when I was young, and I painted my face as well. I recommend a good light weight pair of gloves in a good camo pattern. They need not perfectly match all your camo, but should conceal your hands and blend in with the terrain. You need something with a non-slip grip, like a rubber coating or rubber dots in the palm. That helps you hold your gun securely. Gloves are reasonably cheap, and I have lots of them. I like the gloves I wear to extend up my arm past my shirt sleeve. I pull my shirt sleeve down over them, or pull them over the shirt sleeve, depending on the design of the glove. The long cuffs help to effectively conceal your hands, and help keep bugs like mosquitoes and gnats off your hands. If it is cold you need gloves to keep your hands warm, but they should not be so bulky that they interfere with your handling a call or shooting. I have several pairs that are insulated with Thinsulate material. Thinsulate is warm, but not bulky. Wool works well, if it has something to give you a grip—wool gloves are slick if the palm and fingers are not coated with rubber dots or something. Gloves that include GORE-TEX, in combination with Thinsulate insulation, will help keep your hands warm and dry. Just remember, if you use a friction call or box call, you will need to use your hands. You don't want gloves that will interfere with your using a call. In colder weather I often wear a pair of good warm gloves as I move around from area to area, and then switch to some thinner gloves when I set up and start calling. I also recommend you keep an extra pair of gloves in your vest. I have lost many, many gloves, usually just one of the pair, but you need both. I also keep an extra head-net or two in my vest. They are likewise easy to lose.

HEADNETS / FACEMASKS AND HATS

You need a head-net/facemask that matches your other camo reasonably well. It does not have to be a perfect match, but you don't want anything that contrasts with your other camo enough to draw attention. I like one that goes completely over my head and comes down to my shoulders, covering my hair, face, and neck. I can then wear a hat or can leave it off if it is really hot. A half or three-quarters mask is fine, as long as it conceals you well. These style masks must of course be used with a hat. I prefer these style masks to have the wire frame around the opening for my eyes and across the nose, so I can adjust it over the bridge of my nose and around my eyes to cover well and to give me good peripheral vision—you want nothing obstructing your view. Turkeys have excellent vision, so I don't like to leave anything uncovered, and I mean anything. When hunting, you want to scan the area by moving your eyes back and forth, not by moving your head. Occasionally I will purchase a head-net or facemask that restricts my peripheral vision more than I can tolerate. Those often end up in my turkey vest as extras, just in case I need them, or I give them to someone who goes hunting with me and has no facemask. I prefer a thin facemask that does not restrict my hearing. I also like to wear a camo bandana around my neck. It cuts the chill in cool weather, keeps the sun off in hot weather, keeps mosquitoes and gnats from coming in the bottom of your facemask/head-net, conceals your neck, and I have used my bandana as a make-shift facemask when I forgot or lost my facemask. You can also wet a bandana and put it around your neck to cool you off in hot weather. I do not recommend those facemasks or head-nets that have a thin netting and no holes to see through—so-called see-through nets. In dim light, it is hard to see through them. As far as a hat, I wear baseball style caps, boonie hats, and beanies/skull caps. Each has advantages and disadvantages. The baseball style caps are generally the coolest, and I wear them often in hot weather, particularly those with mesh on the back rather than solid material. The boonie hat in my view does a better job of breaking up your outline, and is a little warmer for colder temps. The brim extends around the whole hat and keeps stuff from falling down your neck, and even helps some in a light rain. A narrow brim is preferable because it does not get in your way so much when you lean back against a tree. A wide brim will get in your way and make noise when you turn your head from side to side if you are leaning against a tree. For this reason I don't like the cowboy style camo hat. In open country, they might be okay, but not in the woods. I like the skull caps for warmth (fleece or micro-fleece), but they have no brim, so I carry a fold up baseball style cap in my vest that I can put on when the sun starts to get in my eyes and restrict my vision.

CHAPTER 3
Vests, Decoys, Blinds and other Accessories

TURKEY VESTS

I consider the turkey vest to be essential gear for turkey hunting. Most everyone I know that turkey hunts uses a turkey vest, a fanny pack, or regular pack. Primos makes something it calls a "Freak Seat" that is kind of a combination seat and pack. You have many choices besides a conventional turkey vest. In my view the turkey vest is one of the greatest tools invented for turkey hunting. There were none when I started turkey hunting, and I stuffed calls and such in whatever pockets I had in my pants, shirt, or coat. You will find over time that you accumulate a lot of gear that you want to carry with you when you hunt, thus you will likely want a turkey vest. My vest with contents probably weighs 15 or 20 lbs. I carry calls (several), extra gloves, extra masks, shells, a ratchet pruner, a knife, a compass, an ink pen, latex gloves, plastic ziplock bags, chalk for my box calls, sandpaper for friction calls, decoys, a water bottle, and more. I guess you can understand why I carry and recommend a turkey vest. It also has a good cushion attached to keep my butt dry, and to provide comfort when sitting on the ground. I recommend you get one with plenty of pockets. I like pockets that have zippers, so I can open and close them without lots of noise, and so stuff does not fall out.

Velcro is noisy, and a pocket without a closing mechanism of some sort is a lost call waiting to happen. You want pockets designed to hold box calls (long pockets), pockets for friction calls and strikers, pockets for mouth calls (you need to have them in some case or such to protect them and keep them clean), pockets with shell loops for extra shells, and pockets for the other things you might want to carry. I like a vest with pockets on the inside and out and with big pockets and small. A padded back helps when you sit up against trees or rocks. You sometimes must sit still for a long while, and that padded back really helps. In my view, a large game bag on the back is a must. I seldom use it to carry dead turkeys, but do use it to carry collapsible (foam or folding) turkey decoys, my water bottle, extra clothes, rain suit, etc.—the decoys provide padding for the back when not in use to decoy a turkey. A thick, comfortable seat cushion that attaches and detaches easy is desirable, and it should not be noisy when you move around on it. It should be water proof and clean up easy. Mine gets turkey blood on it when I carry a turkey over my back (feet up and head down), and it cleans up easy with the garden hose or in a creek or puddle. Long story short, to me a turkey vest is an essential piece of equipment, and you want to get one that suits you. Look around at different ones and you will see the different designs. I have four, but only one is my favorite, and I feel naked without it. If I take one of my others, I cannot locate stuff quickly like I can with my favorite vest. You can find turkey vests at prices ranging from $20 to $200. You can usually get a pretty good one for $40 to $75.

On left is my favorite vest with its many zippered compartments, inside and out. On the right are my light-weight vest with shoulder straps and a fanny pack with plenty of storage compartments. Both are good for hunting in hot weather.

DECOYS

Decoys are legal in most states but not all. They come in various styles, shapes, sizes and materials. I would summarize them as follows: rigid body decoys, foam body decoys, flat or nearly flat (silhouette) decoys, and inflatable decoys. Rigid body (hard plastic) or semi-rigid (softer flexible plastic) decoys tend to look very real and perform well, but they can be bulky, hard to carry, and noisy. I have an old hard plastic decoy which was the first one I ever bought—nothing else was available at that time. I named her "lucky clucker." That old hen looked very good and still does, but I never use it because it is just too noisy and bulky. I have several of the softer plastic decoys that will fold up a little for carrying them, and they are not so noisy. I have two such hens, one posed in the feeding position and one in the breeding position, and three gobbler decoys. Two of the gobbler decoys are mature gobblers that you can put a real feather fan on to make them look and act more realistic as a breeze moves them about. Their carefully painted heads and taxidermy eyes make them look so real, I nearly shot one when I woke up from an unplanned nap. I have a jake decoy made of the same material as the mature gobblers and it also works well. The silk fans that come with them work well, though not as well as a real gobbler fan, but they are much easier to carry in your turkey vest because they fold up. I use a real fan (dried flat and spread as in the strut) sometimes when I know I am going to be driving right up to where I will set up my decoys. For the B-Mobile Gobbler and Jake—I have both—Primos designed a folding base into which you can slip real gobbler tail feathers. It folds up nicely and looks better than a silk fan, but not as good as a dried full fan.

Foam decoys like those made by Flambeau, Delta, and FeatherFlex are light weight, fold up nicely, look alright, and work pretty well if it is not too windy. A hard wind will have them looking like a turkey doing an Irish Jig—not too realistic. I have used them in strong wind and steadied them by sticking another stake or a stick in the ground beside their tail to keep them from spinning round and round. I almost always have one of these foam decoys in my vest, simply because they are so light, compact, and easy to carry. Flat decoys, like the Montana decoys, can be effective, and they look very lifelike from the front or back. As you can guess, they don't look like much from the side view. In open country where the direction of a turkeys approach is pretty predictable, they can be very effective. Used correctly, they can bring in turkeys. Inflatable decoys, like Sceery decoys, are a good choice when you hunt in areas accessible only by a long hike. They are compact, and light, so you can carry 3 or 4 of them in your turkey vest, along with their stakes, and hardly know they are there. Twenty plus years ago I bought a blow up turkey decoy that laced up to a stick or something to hold it up. It looked good as far as color and shape, but was a pain in the rear to use. It never really would stand up in lifelike manner. Sceery was the innovator that made the inflatable decoys practical by designing a mechanism to attach them to a plastic stake that was simple and would allow you to position the decoys so that they looked real. They don't look as lifelike as some of the other decoys, but they do work. No decoy is going to work all the time. I use the Sceery decoys when I hunt Merriam turkeys in South Dakota and Northeast Nebraska because they are very light, and I make long hikes into where I hunt. The Sceery decoy color looks much like a Merriam, which is a plus in those areas. The downside of the inflatable decoys is that you have to blow them up to use them, and squeeze the air out of them to put them away. It can be a little time consuming, but overall, they are not a bad decoy choice.

Gobbler decoys can be very effective, and all of mine, including the jake, move around and look quite real with a slight breeze to cause movement. I have seen gobblers come running to these decoys and even jump on them. The jake is probably a safe bet most of the time, because nearly any gobbler will want to come check him out. Two year olds might be intimidated by the mature gobbler decoys and shy away. I usually set out a couple of hens with my gobbler decoys, but sometimes use only one or two hens and no gobblers. Numerous factors go into the decision about what decoys to use and how to use them. I will say more about how to use them later. If you are hunting public land, gobbler decoys should be used with caution if used at all.

Never set them up where someone might shoot you if they shoot at your decoy. It can happen, so think safety first!

Decoy spread: includes a mature gobbler, a hen in the breeding position, and a feeding hen off to the side. All are molded rubber, so they are light and will fold for storage. The gobbler's fan is a real Rio fan. Note: a gobbler comes out of the strut to breed a hen.

BLINDS

Blinds are useful in some situations. I have two of them. One of them is an inexpensive one man blind, and the other is a two man blind. Both are pop-up style blinds and set up and take down pretty quick and easy. They are very helpful for bow hunting turkeys as they conceal your movement very effectively, and they are quite helpful when you are taking inexperienced adult hunters or kids, for the same reason—the blind conceals their movement. The camo pattern, like your clothing, should be suitable for the environment where you hunt. I like to set my blind up under a tree, or in some brush, then brush it in a little (put brush around it to break up its outline and make it blend in more effectively). Whether or not the blind will spook turkeys has much to do with any previous encounters they may have had with hunters in blinds. Turkeys will sometimes ignore the presence of a blind in the middle of an open field, and other times, they will take a look, get nervous, and then leave even a concealed blind.

I use a blind most often when it is raining or threatening rain. While my blinds are not "rain proof," they shed water reasonably well and keep me drier than I would be sitting under a tree or out in the open. They leak a little at the seams, but it is tolerable. Some blinds are actually water proof, but they tend to be more expensive. I have sat in my two man blind through torrential downpours and hail storms (nickel sized hail—bigger hail might be dangerous) and stayed pretty dry.

I use my blinds for deer hunting as well, so they are not just for turkey hunting. You can also buy small blinds that set up on stakes or pop up, and are only about 18 inches to 2 feet high and 3 to 6 feet long. They provide additional concealment and can be handy also. You can buy a blind at prices ranging from $40 to $400. You need not spend a lot of money to get a pretty good blind. If you use a regular size blind, you will need chairs. I have some folding chairs, like you can buy in Wal-Mart for $10. Mine came as a pair with a Ford Explorer some years ago, and both fit in a single carry bag with a shoulder strap. A newer style of blind you will see advertised is the chair blind. They look good, but I have not used one. They look to me like they would be hard to move around in and that would be a disadvantage if a turkey came up from an unexpected direction—you cannot really get up and turn around. Their obvious advantage is combining two pieces of equipment in one. Hub style blinds generally offer plenty of room and can be set up and taken down quickly, but they tend to be heavier and more bulky. Most blinds come with some sort of bag and straps for carrying them. Carrying blind, chair(s), a gun, vest, decoys, etc. can be a bit much. It is nice to have help, or to be able to drive to the spot you intend to hunt, set things up, and then go park the vehicle and walk back to the blind for the hunt. You need not have a blind to start turkey hunting; however, if you turkey hunt a lot and plan to hunt with a bow and/or take others with you, a suitable blind would be a good investment. As with a vest, there are many styles, sizes and camo patterns available. A little shopping is advisable so that you get the most for your money.

OTHER ACCESSORIES

In my opinion a pruning tool (pruners) for cleaning out a spot to sit down is an essential tool. I did it with a knife for many years, and still carry a fixed blade Marine combat knife which I occasionally use on large limbs. Pruners make it easy and quiet to clean out a spot to set up. Many different styles are available, but as long as the tool does the job for you, it's good. I have one pruner that was $2 on sale at a hardware store, and another that was around $20. I have seen some for as much as $85, but I would never pay that much myself. My $20 pruner is a ratchet pruner and will cut limbs up to an inch in diameter without much difficulty, although I seldom need that kind of cutting power. Generally, I am just cutting briars, vines, limbs, and small saplings. You can buy pruners in sporting goods stores, hardware stores, and more. My favorite pruner is very compact, black, costs $5 on sale (no brand name), and will cut limbs up to ½ inch diameter without a problem. Being small, it fits in my vest quite nicely and it does the job. I use it to cut stuff in the way before I sit down, and after I sit down to clear stuff that might obstruct my view or get in the way of my gun if I need to move around. I sometimes clear out brush all the way around a tree, in case I have to reposition myself for a turkey approaching from behind.

Folding or rigid seats can be helpful to supplement your turkey vest cushion, or to substitute for it. I have several such seats, but two are particularly noteworthy. One of my favorites is about 12 by 16 inches in size, made of aluminum with a green finish, has strong and quiet camo webbing for the seat, has adjustable legs (back legs longer than front legs), and an adjustable carry strap. This one is real handy for hunting in the mountains or very hilly terrain. If you set up on the side of a hill, you can extend or shorten the legs to whatever extent is necessary to give yourself a flat surface on which to sit. It can be very uncomfortable to sit on the side of a steep incline, and it is hard to stay still and maintain stability for a good shot without the aid of a seat like this one. I would not hunt the Black Hills of SD without it. It is also handy in places where you need a little bit of extra elevation to see over tall grass or vegetation. I found it to be quite useful in Texas, Kansas and Nebraska to enable me to see over the grass and ground cover. I have a second seat that I really like as well. It is a short camo seat with a back on it—essentially a short folding chair—and it has a carry strap. The one I use is sold by Cabela's and is called a Gobbler Lounger. I use it in open country where it is hard to find a good set up with a back rest—if you don't have something to lean against, you get uncomfortable real quick. I can sit comfortably for hours in that seat. I have set up using that seat in tall grass, backed into a hole I cut for myself at the edge of a plumb thicket, and set up with it in blow-downs. The Gobbler Lounger helps me to hide and sit comfortably. Similar seats are available from other companies besides Cabela's. I don't use either of these seats all the time, but I use them when I need them. Having done without them, I appreciate very much the comfort, stability, and improved visibility that they give me in certain situations.

I carry a small, light weight knife in my vest to breast a turkey if I am way back in the mountains or deep the woods, and don't want to have to carry the whole bird out. That is illegal is some places, so know the game laws and whether or not it is legal. That is also why I carry zip lock bags and latex gloves. By using the latex gloves, your hands don't get messy, and latex decomposes rather quickly and does not harm the environment if you dispose of them in the woods—sunlight breaks them down. Plastic gloves do not decompose, so if you use them, carry them out with you. The knife can also come in handy for other things. It is the only knife I use to dress turkeys in the woods or out, and I keep it very sharp. Because it stays in my vest, I always know where it is located.

CHAPTER 3: VESTS, DECOYS, BLINDS, AND OTHER ACCESSORIES • 23

For comfort when sitting: Cabela's Gobbler Lounger and a Buckwing fold up seat with adjustable legs. Other gear from author's turkey vest includes: Eucalyptus and Lemon insect spray, compact headlamp, cell phone, pruner, sunglasses, coyote call, peacock call, extra gloves, binoculars, compass, Opinel light-weight folding knife, and bola water bottle.

Other things I carry in my vest and recommend you include in yours include the following: matches (water proof) or lighter, extra shells, ink pen for filling out tags if required, and string for attaching turkey tags if required. If you are hunting big woods where getting lost is a possibility, carrying a compass or GPS is a good idea. I also carry my cell phone in case of emergency, although it does not work in many of the remote places I hunt. I of course put it on vibrate when I am hunting. On occasion, my buddies and I use two-way radios (ones that can be set on vibrate) so we can communicate with each other. On more than one occasion, I spotted for my buddy Tim as he moved closer to turkeys, and we used the radios to communicate. Radios are prohibited by law in some states, so be sure you know the regulations. I also carry a good pair of compact binoculars when hunting in the mountains or in open country. They can come in handy in determining whether turkeys at a distance are gobblers or hens before you walk a long ways to get close enough to hunt them. I also carry a water bottle. I sometimes hunt all day, and I must have water, a sport drink, or something. I have a bota bottle (two in fact—gifts from my buddy Tim) that is made of plastic (safe and flexible milk jug plastic—no BPAs), and has a black nylon cover with an adjustable shoulder strap. This style of bota bottle is reasonably quiet and durable, and it holds over 20 ounces of liquid. There are plenty of choices available for water bottles, but I want something fairly quiet, not shiny, streamline, and safe—not a plastic that will give me cancer and react with something besides water that I might decide to put in it! The bota bottle fits the bill for me. I tried a couple of bota wine skins made of leather, but the plastic bladders inside of them were prone to rupture if you sat on them or something stuck in them, and they tended to give the water a bad taste. You can of course just stick a plastic bottle of "spring" water from the store in your bag, but don't leave the bottle in the woods. Those plastic bottles don't decompose quickly when left in the woods, and they can be noisy when partially or completely empty. Last, I usually carry some sort of snacks in my turkey vest. Some peanut butter crackers or a granola bar can taste really good when you are hungry!

CHAPTER 4
THE TURKEY GUN AND RELATED ACCESSORIES

It is perfectly alright to use a general purpose shotgun for turkey hunting, but you should be mindful of the choke and the loads you shoot. You need a good pattern because you want to be able to kill birds out to 40 or 45 yards. That is no problem with the right choke and loads, and is pretty routine for a good turkey gun. Many turkeys are killed further than that, but if you do your homework and set up properly, shorter shots should be the norm for you. I used a general purpose gun when I started turkey hunting, largely because I could not afford another gun, but now I use a "turkey gun." I would not like to hunt with any other gun, because I have great faith in my turkey gun. It is an old Remington 870, 12 gauge, Super Mag, Turkey gun. It came with a Remington "super full" turkey choke that produced a good tight pattern. My gun only shoots 3 inch magnum loads—they did not have 3 ½ inch loads back when I bought it. I know many hunters who prefer guns chambered for 3 ½ inch shells, but mine kicks hard enough already. I don't feel the need to shoot heavier loads. To each his own! I eventually put a Kicks aftermarket choke on my gun after trying several brands without being impressed enough to replace the old Remington choke. With the Kicks choke, the gun patterns very, very well with recommended Winchester Supreme number 5 shot. The choke was matched by the manufacturer with my gun and the shells, taking into consideration barrel length, etc. The forcing cone was also modified on my gun by a local gunsmith to improve the pattern. This simple process is relatively inexpensive. The shells were recommended by the choke manufacturer, but they were already my preferred shells. There are many other good aftermarket chokes available, and you can pay less than I paid, or you can pay much more. The choice depends largely on your needs, your pocket book, and what works best for you. My gun has a short barrel, which I prefer. The shorter barrel is nice when you are set up and have to swing on the bird. With the shorter barrel, you are less apt to hit something with the barrel as you move the gun. I have friends who prefer longer barrels. One of my best turkey hunting buddies likes the longer barrel because his vision has changed with age, and he says he can sight better down that long barrel. Others I know with similar vision issues have opted to use scopes on their guns with shorter barrels to solve the problem. To each his own! My 870 is of course a pump, but autoloaders are popular as well. I have nothing against an autoloader. They work just fine to get that follow up shot if needed, just like a pump, only a little faster. Some hunters use double barrels, and some single shots. My first turkey gun was my Dad's old double barrel LC Smith 12 gauge. I killed turkeys with it, but it was a bit heavy and not very maneuverable. My first serious "turkey gun" was an old H&R 10 gauge. I killed lots of turkeys with it, but it was very heavy—like toting a small cannon. There are many, many good choices for turkey guns. You can buy an 870 Super Mag with a black composite stock for a little over $300, or you can spend upwards of $1600 for something like a Benelli autoloader. I have friends that have the Benelli turkey guns and love them. You can shoot factory loads like I do (around $10 for a box of 10), or buy high dollar custom heavy shot loads for $8 a shell (that is for 3 ½ inch shells), like some of my friends prefer. Quite frankly, I think I miss fewer birds with my gun than some of my buddies do with their high dollar guns and high dollar loads. Your gun should not be easily spotted by a turkey. A shiny finish is not a good thing. If you use a gun with such a finish, cover it with a gun sock or chaps, or some camo tape—they make tape that will cover it, stay on, and not mar the finish of your gun. If you buy a turkey gun, flat black or camo are pretty much standard colors. Mine is black, but nearly all my buddies have guns with camo finishes. Does it make a difference whether it is black or camo? I really don't think I have been busted by many turkeys because of my black gun. When I get another, I may buy one in camo. When I bought mine, it was not available. In fact, my turkey gun had a wooden stock and black mat finish on the barrel. I promptly painted the stock and forearm flat black. Now, some of the brown shows, but it still seems to do pretty well. I bought another 870 some years back for an "extra" and it is flat black with a black composite stock. I have yet take to it in the woods, but might do so one day if my old Turkey gun ever wears out.

If you are outfitting a young child with a turkey gun, I think you would be well advised to go with a 20 gauge and 3 inch shells. Different manufacturers make turkey loads for these guns. Remington makes an 870 youth model turkey gun that is essentially a scaled down version of my 870 turkey gun. I bought one for my son when he was about 8 or 9 and he killed his first turkey with it at about 25 yards. He also used it for rabbits, squirrels, and such. The 870 is not expensive, and there are many other brands to choose from as well. Some will cost more and some less. If you are really on a tight budget, a single shot will do. You can allow a child to practice with 2 ¾ inch shells to become proficient with the gun, and use the turkey loads for hunting. If you don't want the child to get scared of the kick (could cause them to flinch at the moment of truth), you can pattern the gun yourself with the turkey loads to know what it will do. Turkey loads kick a little harder, but if the child is shooting at a turkey, he/she will not likely even feel the kick—too excited to notice. Number 5 or number 6 shot will probably work best for turkeys—you have a fairly dense pattern, and good enough shock with this shot size. The youth gun is also a good choice for a small woman, as it has a short stock, short reach to the fore end, and is essentially designed for a "small" person.

Regardless of what gun you use, you need to know your gun and you accomplish that by patterning the gun. Getting advice from people who use the same gun can save you some money on shells, in terms of what works best. If you don't know anyone, check out the Web. You can find plenty of advice on hunting forums. Everybody has an opinion! Long story short, you need to shoot the gun, see how it patterns, become proficient with it, and perhaps most importantly, know its limitations. Most misses and crippled birds are the result of taking a bad shot, or not knowing the gun's or your own limitations. Practice does truly make perfect. You can buy targets that have the upper body, neck, and head of a turkey on them for realism, or just draw something pretty close. I recommend you use a piece of news paper, or some other similar sized paper or cardboard for a back drop so you can evaluate the whole pattern. Pattern the gun at 20, 30, 40 and 50 yards to know what it will do. I am not saying to shoot at turkeys at 50 yards, but you must know the capabilities of your gun. Know also, that it will pattern differently with different shot sizes, and even with different manufacturer's loads of the same size shot and powder charge. Remember also, that the downside of a tight pattern is that it is very tight at short range. At 10 yards it is likely smaller than the diameter of a baseball, so you must take that into consideration. When a bird is really close, I shoot at the base of its neck because a bobbing head is a difficult target. I have missed at 5 yards! The base of the neck is not nearly so difficult a target—does not move around a lot—when you are pulling the trigger at close range. Yes, you might ruin a little meat, but you will have a better chance of getting your turkey. How many pellets should you have in the head and neck area to be effective? Different people have different opinions, but for me 20 to 40 pellets in the head and neck is good—not on the edge, but in the kill zone (spine and brain areas). If you can do that with your gun consistently, then you should be able to kill turkeys with it.

As far as a sight on your gun, different people like different sight setups. I have a small fiber optic bead on the end of my barrel, and an even smaller metal bead half-way down the barrel (mounted on the rib). I like that set up as it helps me get a good tight aim on a turkey. With a tight choke, you must aim carefully, not just point and shoot. Some like shotgun scopes of various sorts, and some like something akin to rifle sights on their turkey gun. What matters most is whether the sight setup on your gun works for you. There have been times when I pulled a trigger on a bird right off the roost early in the morning, when there was not much daylight. Take that into consideration when you evaluate your sights. You don't want to miss an opportunity in low light because you never gave it a thought when selecting a sight for your gun.

If you hunt long hours and cover a lot of ground like most hunters I know do, you will want a sling on your gun. I recommend you equip your gun with a good sling that won't slide off your shoulder when you are walking. Neoprene slings seem to work well, and have the advantage of being quiet as well. That is what I have on nearly all my guns. A sling is really handy when you have to walk into an area you will hunt carrying a seat, blind, or other equipment in addition to the gun, and/or will be carrying a turkey out. That the sling does not slip is particularly important to me, because it is a pain to have to stop and pull the gun back up on your shoulder if you are hauling a load. I sometimes wrap the sling over my knee when set up, to help me keep the gun up without having it rest right on top of my knee—having the gun on top of the knee can make the knee sore after a long sit. I have a friend who always takes his strap off when he sets up, because he says it gets in his way. Quick detach swivels are a plus.

CHAPTER 5
TURKEY CALLS

There are many different styles of turkey calls. Most reproduce turkey sounds by friction or by air movement. Box calls, pot and striker calls, push box calls, scratch box calls, etc. employ friction between two surfaces to produce a sound like a turkey. Diaphragm calls, tube calls, squeeze calls, and trumpet style/wingbone calls all employ some form of air movement to produce sounds. The choices are many and varied when it comes to turkey calls.

BOX CALLS

There are many different box call styles to choose from. Some are short and compact and some are long, like the boat paddle style box calls. Box calls are made using different types of wood and some employ synthetic materials. You can get one for as little as $10 and you can pay hundreds for custom box calls. As a general rule, the larger the call is, the greater the volume. I personally prefer a walnut or cedar box call, but I have heard many other box calls of other materials that sounded great. Seems to me, with any reasonably good quality box call, the main determinant of the quality of the sound that comes from it is the user. I own two Lynch World Champion box calls. One is my first "bought" turkey call (it's 43 years old and still sounds great), and the other is the one I carry hunting, my new one (it only 25 years old). The World Champion Box call, or the Lynch "Fool Proof" box call, is a good choice for the beginner or the expert. I have various assorted custom box calls, but I still prefer my Lynch to any of the rest. With it I can gobble, yelp, cluck, whine, putt, purr and cackle. That is all I need to do! There are many choices available, and I am not about to tell you which one you should buy. You need to try them out, and see how you like them. You want to get one that sounds good, is reasonably easy to use and maintain, and will fit in your turkey vest. I have a great sounding call that David Blanton gave me years ago. It was custom made by M.L. Ashley of Alabama from a solid piece of red cedar. The problem with it is that the thing is huge—over a foot long, 3 to 4 inches deep, and nearly 2 inches wide. While it sounds great, it is just too big to carry with me in my turkey vest. I have another boat paddle style box call that my buddy Emory gave me for Christmas one year. It is called a Scott's Cutter and is made by Jake Scott. It is a little long, but it is a great cutting call prospect calling—the sound seems to carry forever! I find it a little awkward to do soft yelps with it. Long story short, a box call is a good choice for the novice or the expert looking for a little different sound. It is easy for the beginner to make basic yelps and clucks with a box. Many turkeys have been killed using just those two sounds, but in the hands of an accomplished caller, the box provides the means of faithfully reproducing a wide range of turkey sounds.

Because the lid of a box call moving across the call produces sound whether intended or not, I recommend you put a rubber band or something around it to keep it from squeaking when you walk or move around. Placing something between the lid and sound chamber can accomplish the same end, but it may remove the chalk from the lid and edges.

Box Calls: From left to right a Scott's Cutter, Pen Woods Mini Boat Paddle, Lynch World Champion Box Call, custom box call by Larry Greathouse of Arkansas, and custom box call by M. L. Ashley of Alabama. On bottom is a call case with call inside.

POT AND STRIKER / FRICTION CALLS

Pot and striker calls are called friction by most folks. A skillful caller can produce nearly every sound in the turkey vocabulary with this call. Strikers are made from various materials, with walnut, hickory, and cedar being pretty popular natural materials. Acrylic and carbon are popular synthetic materials. Pots are made of plastic and wood for the most part, with striking surfaces made most often from slate, glass, ceramic, and aluminum. I have one with the striking surface made of wood, but it must to be chalked frequently, and I can never achieve much volume with it. You have many pot and striker combinations to choose from. You can buy an off the shelf model by Primos, Knight and Hale, or HS Strut, in most sporting goods stores for $8 to $20 dollars, or you can pay $40 and up for something like a Cody Custom call. As far as sound quality, it is hard to beat slate—I prefer it. My favorite call is slate over glass, which means the surface I strike is slate, but it has glass in the pot under the slate to vibrate, thus enhancing the sound quality. Holes in the bottom allow sound to exit the sound chamber. The bad thing about slate, is that it requires frequent conditioning (touching up the surface with sandpaper, steel wool, or some other mildly abrasive material) and it does not work well when wet. Glass works well, produces a good sound, and with a glass or carbon striker it works when wet. Several call companies produce calls made from a ceramic material that produces a sound comparable to slate. Ceramic surfaces can also be used when wet, if matched with the right striker. Aluminum calls work well to produce the high pitch sounds of a hen turkey. Any surface requires some conditioning; my slate requires the most and my ceramic requires the least.

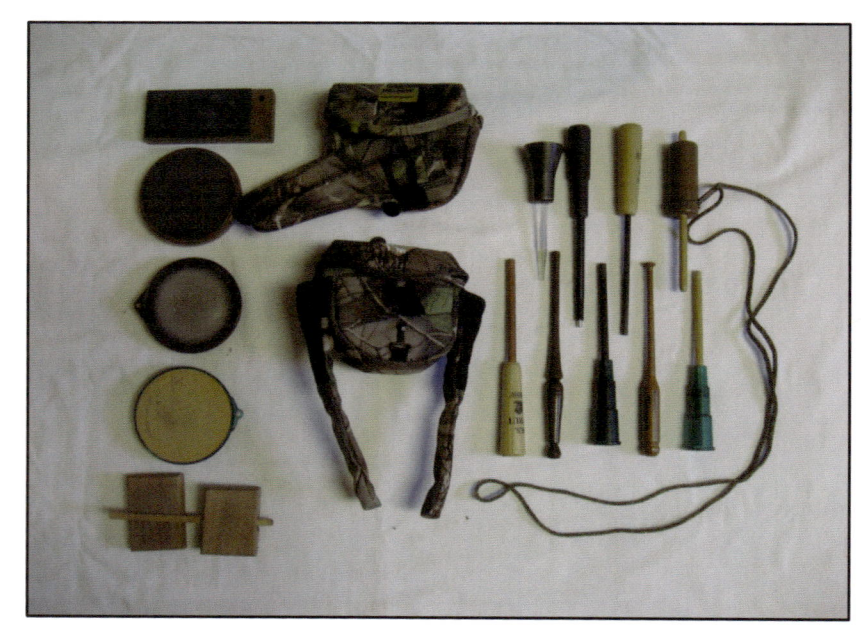

On left from top to bottom: Bill Harper slate by Lohman, custom slate by Larry Greathouse, H.S. Strut Black Magic Aluminum, Knight and Hale Ol' Yeller Sla-tec (ceramic), and a custom friction call made of walnut. In the middle are two call cases. On the right is an assortment of strikers including glass (actually acrylic), aluminum, carbon, and wood. Cedar, rosewood, cocobolo, hickory, and walnut are commonly used in strikers as are many other exotic and laminated woods.

Nearly everyone I know prefers one or the other of the surfaces described and has a favorite call and striker. I have two or three of each kind, but I use my slate and my aluminum calls more than any other. It is just a matter of personal preference. I use different strikers with different surfaces. My favorite strikers are made of cocobolo wood, ebony, walnut and hickory. I use cedar and glass strikers on occasion. You can spend a lot of money on some of the fancy laminated custom strikers, but I don't. I am not saying they are not good, but I am saying that I don't think it is necessary. If you are, or you eventually become, a serious turkey hunter, you will certainly end up with various pot and striker combinations, and you will discover what works for you. To get started, just about anything you buy off a store shelf will allow you to practice and learn to make turkey sounds.

DIAPHRAGM CALLS

Diaphragm calls are perhaps the most popular call. I suspect more of them are sold than any other. There are some people, very few, who cannot use them because they gag on them. Most of those folks don't get over that affliction and simply cannot use a diaphragm call. Most seasoned turkey hunters I know use diaphragms at one time or another, if for nothing else but back-up at close range; when the bird gets close, they use it rather than moving their hands to work another style of call. The diaphragm is my favorite style of call because, with a diaphragm call, I can make virtually any call a turkey can make, including a gobble (I am not as good as some at producing a gobble, but I can do it). Most importantly, it allows hand free operation which allows me to minimize movement and keep my hands on my gun. There are many, many styles of diaphragm calls around, and I would not think of telling you which is best. Size, shape, materials, tension on the latex, number of layers of latex, latex thickness, cuts in the latex, and the caller, all influence the sound of the call. I honestly don't know two turkey hunters that have the same favorite. I often have friends suggest one to me, and I usually buy and try them, but seldom do I like anyone else's preferred call as well as my own. My favorite call changes over time. I generally like multi reed calls with V cuts or bat-wing cuts. I tend to prefer thinner latex because I can call softly or loud with calls made from multiple layers of thin latex. I never know when I pick up a new diaphragm call whether or not it might become my new favorite, so I am always willing to try something new. I probably have 100 or more in my refrigerator. That is where I keep them because the latex diaphragm deteriorates with heat, and it deteriorates rapidly in sunlight. Don't leave them sitting in the sun. When I do find one I like, I buy several of them and put them up. Like just about everything now-a-days, companies will phase out the old to make room for the new. You may not be able to get more in the future, so stock up. My favorite at present is a 3 reed raspy hen produced by Southern Game calls. I had three, and I am now down to my last one.

Assorted diaphragm calls and cases. Various cuts, reed combinations, and tuning will result in very different sounds for diaphragm calls. A call case protects your calls in the field. If you wash them before storing them, they will last longer.

Diaphragm calls are easy to use, but difficult to master—to make all the turkey sounds very well. My college roommate Carlton showed me how to make them, and my first one was made from a beer can that I cut up with tin snips. I doubled a flat piece over and cut out a horseshoe shaped piece. It might have been the size of a quarter. I used that, a condom for latex, and some of the old white medical tape to make my first diaphragm call. That was before you could buy one. My homemade diaphragms were not very sophisticated or durable, but they worked. Now

I buy them and I always carry 4 to 6 in my call pouch (protects them). I also have several more stored away in my vest, just in case I lose my call pouch. It has happened and it can ruin your day! Carry extras in your vest or in your truck, just in case.

You make sound with diaphragm calls by forcing air across the surface of the diaphragm which you hold against the roof of your mouth with your tongue. Tongue movement, pressure, air flow control, and mouth movement all influence the sound. It is really impossible to tell you in words precisely how to make turkey sounds with a diaphragm call, so I won't try. Most come with instructions. That can help, but it is best to get a skilled caller to show you how, or to watch instructional videos. You can even find resources on the web to help you learn to use a diaphragm call. On the Web you can find written instructions, videos, audios clips, etc. to help you get started. Watching hunting videos is a good way to learn what turkeys sound like.

SCRATCH BOX CALLS

Scratch box calls are some great sounding turkey sounds, but they require a high level of skill to master. The two surfaces are normally wood, and it is entirely up to the caller to hold them (the striker in one hand and box in the other) the exact right way and produce the exact right movement to produce the desired sound. I don't recommend them for beginners. I have several, but seldom use them. For me, they are more of a novelty.

PUSH BOX CALLS

Push box calls are very easy to use and very forgiving (forgiving of mistakes) for the beginner. Some are made of wood, and some are made of plastic. Both materials can produce good yelps and clucks. They basically move a wood or plastic peg over a wood, aluminum, or slate surface inside the box to make the sounds. A skilled caller can produce a variety of calls with push box calls, but they are designed primarily for beginners and for ease of use. I have a couple, but I never use them for hunting. For the beginner, they are not a bad choice. David Hale, who is no beginner, uses a push box call is some of his videos. I am not sure if it is because he really likes the push box call, or because he sells them. Either way, he calls up lots of turkeys with push box calls.

SQUEEZE CALLS/GOBBLING TUBES

What I call squeeze calls are rubber tubes, with a latex diaphragm in the end, that are designed to produce turkey sounds. Most are for shaking to produce a gobble, but can be squeezed quickly or slowly to produce clucks and yelps. When my son was about 4 years old he had one that he played with all the time. I also had wild turkeys in a pen in my back yard. I heard yelping outside the window of the house one day and thought one of my hens had somehow escaped from the pen. I ran outside to check only to find my son sitting in the shade under a window playing with that squeeze call. It fooled me, and I think it can fool a turkey. If a 4 year old can make a convincing yelp with a squeeze call, just about anyone should be able to use it!

TUBE CALLS

Tube calls are not very common. Some custom call manufacturers make them, but you don't typically find them in stores. Few hunters master and use this style of call. The reason is simple; it is not real easy to master the tube call. They are kind of a specialty call like the wingbone. My first tube call was made from a snuff box, and I don't mean a Skoal or Copenhagen box. Powdered snuff came in a metal cylinder 2 to 4 inches long and about an inch and a half in diameter. We made tube calls by cutting out half the bottom of the snuff can (half moon shape) and stretching latex over the cut out opening, securing it with a rubber band. You blow a tube call kind of like a flute, forcing air over the diaphragm to produce turkey sounds. My first one I used by pushing the latex end up against my top lip to blow—it tickled my lips too much for me to use it effectively. Now, I hold them with the open end facing up and away and push the latex (business end) against my bottom lip. Sounds can be toned down or magnified by how you cup your hand over the open end, and by how hard you blow. Modern tube calls are shaped essentially the same way as our old snuff box calls, but most are turned out of various exotic and domestic woods using lathes. Latex is stretched over the end and secured with o-rings, rubber bands, etc. Some "store bought" commercial tube calls are made of plastic. Tube calls are fairly difficult to master, so I don't recommend them for the beginner. If you are willing to practice, you can make almost all calls of the wild turkey with a tube call. My buddy Emory can make a pretty good gobble with one. I can yelp, cluck, cackle, whine, and purr on one, but that is about it. With some practice, you can make a very realistic hen yelp on a tube call, and with some adjustment to the latex and or the latex position, you can make a gobbler yelp. Like diaphragm calls, the latex must be properly cared for or it will deteriorate. I keep my tube calls stored away from heat and sunlight, and the extra latex for them, I keep in the refrigerator.

WINGBONE / TRUMPET STYLE CALLS

Wing bone or trumpet style calls are perhaps the most difficult call to master. The true wing bone call is probably the oldest turkey call known to man. Wing bone calls were used by the American Indians thousands of years ago. Remains of these calls have been found in excavations of village sites in the Americas. Note that not all trumpet calls are made from wing bones. Some, like the infamous Tom Turpin yelper (a trumpet call), are beautifully made of wood, brass, etc. on lathes. The wood, brass or whatever material, is turned to produce something resembling a miniature clarinet—without the buttons or reed. These calls have a very small opening on the end you put your mouth on, and you don't blow it, but rather you suck air through it with something akin to the action of a kiss. How you position the call against your lips and how you pull or suck on it influences the sound, as does the movement of your hand over the opening at the other end. Trumpet and wing bone calls can be used to make a variety of turkey sounds, including the purr, whine, yelp, cluck, putt, and more. I made my first trumpet style call with a spent shotgun shell with the primer punched out, a short piece of plastic tube, and a test tube stopper on the end from which a small portion of the tube protruded—the end I sucked on to make sounds. I called gobblers with it. I make my own wing bone calls now from wing bones that I save. I know people who won't use one made of anything but hen wing bones, but I think mine made of gobbler wing bones work just fine. I have used them to fool old gobblers that would respond to nothing else—birds that were call shy from being hunted hard. While I feel naked without my wing bone call and won't go hunting without it, I don't recommend the wing bone as a starter call. To master it, you are going to have to practice and practice a lot. Calling in a turkey with something I crafted myself from another turkey, gives me a feeling of accomplishment quite different than I get from doing it with any other call. It's hard to explain to anyone who has not done it!

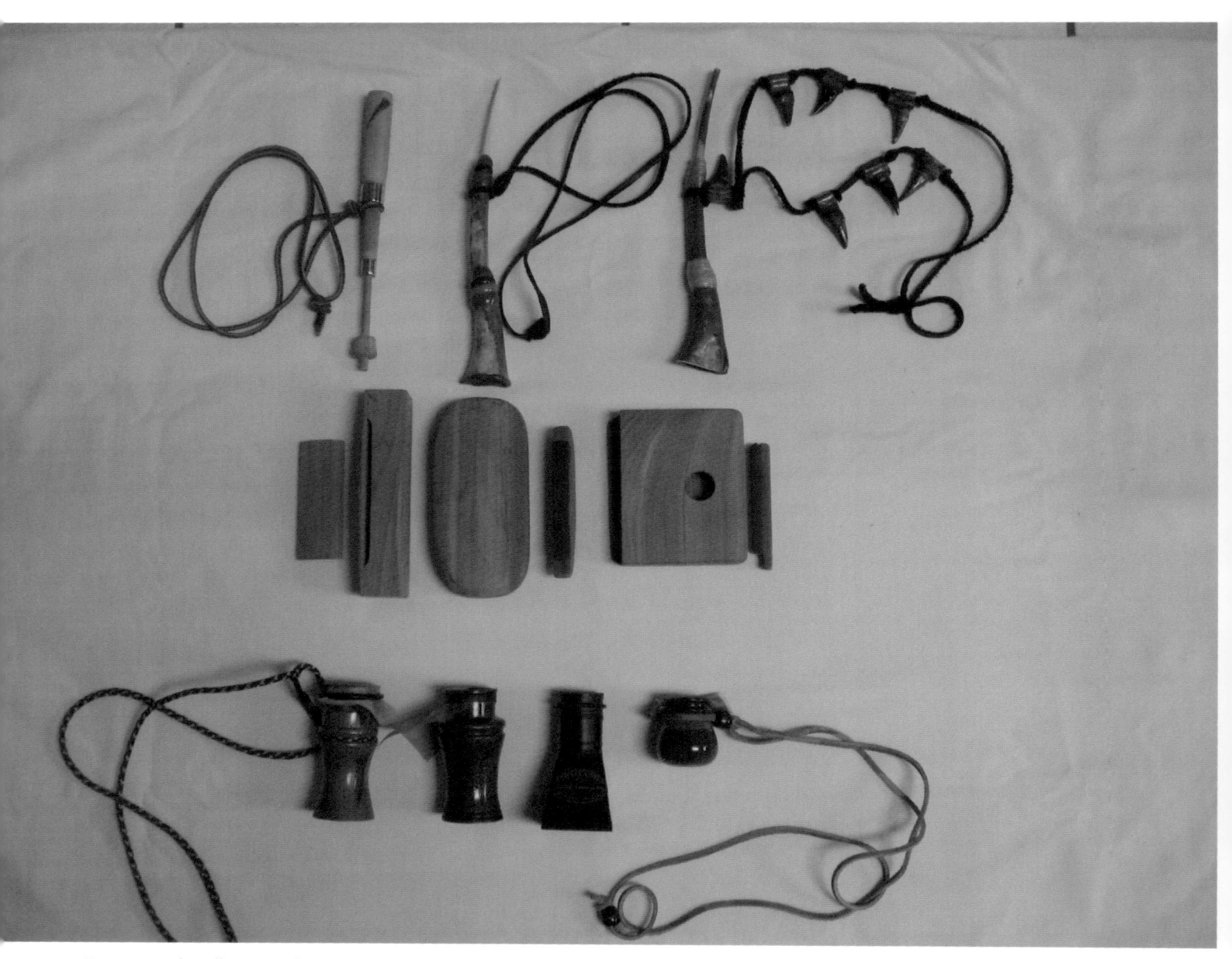

Trumpet style calls across the top including: a bamboo call by Ottis Holland, and two wingbone calls made by the author—the one in the middle the author uses for hunting. Scratch box calls in the middle including: two by Ottis Holland (on either end) and one made by the author (in the center). The scratch-box strikers appear next to the calls and are made from wood, or wood with a slate surface. Tube calls across the bottom are all custom calls, except for the third from the right which is an old Ben Lee Widow Maker.

So, with all these call choices available, what call do you buy? If you are just starting out, I would recommend a friction call (pot and striker type) call, a box call, or a push box call. If you know someone who turkey hunts, get them to recommend something or get them to go with you to pick something out/help you order it online. Most turkey hunters I know love to introduce other hunters to the sport and would love to provide such help—just don't ask them to share their hunting spots. I gave a young man (10 years old) a Primo's friction call this spring. I spent the morning hunting with him and his Dad, both of whom had never hunted turkeys. I let the young man call with me at times and told him what sounded good and what did not. His Dad listened attentively to my instructions to his son. We got a shot but no bird that day. The next day his Dad called in a mature gobbler with that call. The young man killed that old Tom at 20 yards. That is picking it up pretty quick! A box call is a good choice as well, as making yelps and clucks on a box is pretty easy. Be sure to keep it conditioned well (sanded and chalked) to keep it sounding good. A push box is not a bad choice, but most hunters grow out of that call pretty quickly, and move on to the box, diaphragm, or friction call. If you are like me and most of my turkey hunting buddies, you will have at least one of every kind of call, and carry at least a friction call, a box call, multiple diaphragm calls, and perhaps a wing bone call into the woods every time you hunt. Do we use them all? No, but we have them if we need them. I have many calls that I treasure for one reason or another and don't dare take them into the woods—they are not for hunting anymore. Some of them, I only would let you handle if you are "special." Laugh if you want, but I am not the only turkey hunter like that!

CHAPTER 6
A PLACE TO HUNT

If you own your own hunting land, then you are very fortunate. About the next best thing to owning your hunting land is having a good friend or family who will allow you to hunt on their land. I have my own land and access to friends' land, but for me, that is not enough. I don't wish to sound greedy, so I will explain. I do not violate game laws including bag limits. I can only kill two birds in my home state of Arkansas, and when I hunt on friends' land in Georgia, I can only kill three. The good Lord has blessed me with a job that gives me both the time off to hunt during the spring, and the resources I need to hunt many different places. Over time I have hunted more and more places out of state, I have made friends with landowners, so I don't have to actively seek out a place to hunt in many of my destinations. I believe that, if I stay healthy and able to hunt, I will always want to find more places to hunt. Perhaps you will as well. Even if you own your own land, if it is like mine, there may be years when the turkeys are just not staying on your place in the spring. In that case, if you want to hunt, then you have to go elsewhere. I am going to share with you what I have learned about finding both private and public land to hunt.

GETTING PERMISSION TO HUNT PRIVATE LAND
Unless you have turkeys on your own land or family land, you have basically three choices for private land hunting: you can join a hunting club, you can ask permission to hunt on private land, or you can lease some land yourself. There is a fourth I guess, but I hate poachers and poaching so I won't list it here.

For starters, you must know where the turkeys are! If you have lived in an area for a while, you would probably have heard people talk about seeing turkeys, or seen turkeys yourself. Otherwise, it is pretty easy to find out whether or not there are turkeys in an area—you ask! If your interest is primarily is in a place near your home, you can ask at local sporting goods stores, feed stores, etc. You can ask people at work, church, etc. It is also pretty easy to just contact your local game warden and ask him or her. I find that game wardens are typically very willing to help. You can also "Google it" on the Web (Internet). A search phrase like "turkey hunting Yell county Arkansas", or "turkey hunting in Arkansas", can help you locate counties with good turkey populations in your state, or in the state where you intend to hunt. Such searches will often produce links to land for sale, land for lease, turkey population statistics, hunting statistics, and more. In short, the Web puts a world of information at your finger tips, even for such things as a place to turkey hunt.

If you happen to live in, or you are visiting, a small town in rural America, there is almost always a restaurant in town frequented by the "old timers" and farmers from the area. They possess a wealth of valuable knowledge about the area, and they usually like to talk. I have acquired good information about local turkey populations, possible places to hunt, and more, time and time again around the south and Midwest in the local "gathering place." It is not usually hard to find such places. Those restaurants are usually not chains, but instead are mom and pop enterprises, and there's usually many farm trucks in the parking lot early in the morning—that, by the way, is the time to go there! Not only can you find out where turkeys are plentiful from these folks, you might even secure permission to hunt from one of them. I've had more success getting information than getting permission to hunt this way, but it is worth asking for permission to hunt if you get the chance.

Once you know where you can find turkeys in an area, you need to secure permission to hunt. You can ask landowners cold (go up and knock on the door), or you can try to find someone by networking (contacting family or friends of someone you know or met in your quest for a place to hunt). My buddy Tim and I met a lady in a service station in Nebraska one day while getting gas and inquiring at the counter about turkey season dates. She overheard our conversation with the sales clerk, who by the way was clueless. She said her husband was a turkey hunter and he would know the season dates. She went and told her husband about us. He came over while we were gassing up the truck. He introduced himself, told us the season dates, and then proceeded to tell us about an old farmer in the area who had lots of turkeys on his place. He told us how to get to the farmer's house, and even warned us about his temperament (moody). We got permission from the old farmer's wife to hunt, information from his son on where the turkeys were located, went and got our licenses, went back to hunt, and within an hour I had a nice Merriam gobbler hanging up for pictures. While networking usually does not work quite so fast, it is a good way to find hunting places. Networking also can help you to know something about the landowners in advance, like their name, likelihood of securing permission to hunt, and perhaps a little about their overall disposition—it can help.

Whether you have some information about the person in advance, or you are just knocking on someone's door cold, it helps to look presentable. I don't mean suit and tie, but rather neat and clean. If they are country folk, which is usually the case, it is best not to look like a "city slicker," or a "redneck bubba." If you can get their name in advance, that is all the better (like off the mailbox or on the Internet—by using their address). In either case, you just knock on the door or approach them with a smile if they are outside, introduce yourself, shake hands, and then start the conversation. Common courtesy like saying yes sir, no sir, yes mam, no mam, please and thank you, is a plus in my view—tends to make a positive impression on people, particularly country folk. I often comment on what a pretty place they have, or on their dog, horse, cattle, garden, etc. If they have a dog and it does not act mean, I usually pet the dog—same with a cat, goat, horse or whatever pet may be right there. After introducing myself, and a little "ice breaking" conversation, I simply ask if they allow hunting on their land. Sometimes it ends there—they indicate that only family and or friends hunt it, that it is leased, or that they simply don't want anyone hunting on their land. If they indicate they are not open to my hunting their place, I politely thank them and leave. If they don't say no right away, I tell them I am a safe and experienced hunter and then ask if they would mind if I were to turkey hunt on their land. I tell them I will leave no litter, and that I will close gates, drive only where they say to drive, and otherwise take care of their property as if it were my own. If they give me permission to hunt, I then ask them where they would prefer that I park my truck. If I am not in my hunting truck, I tell them what it looks like. Ask permission if you plan on bringing another hunter with you—child, wife or whoever. If you will be in another vehicle, give them a description of it. Ask about land boundaries, any areas they want you to avoid, etc. I normally offer the owner some or all of the turkey I might take on the place. I am more than willing to give owners a turkey breast, or a whole turkey, if they allow me to hunt. You may or may not want to do this—depends on how bad you want the turkey for yourself. If I do give them a turkey or breast, it is meticulously clean and well packaged when I deliver it. People make assumptions about you based on how you do things—right or wrong. I like to do things in a way that leaves people with a positive impression of me.

I have often offered to help with work in trade for permission to hunt. Don't do it, unless you mean it. I do mean it! If I am talking to a farmer and he is working on fence while I am talking to him, filling a planter with corn, or whatever, I will step in there and help if he will allow me to. Don't get in the way or offer to help if you don't know how. I grew up in the country and worked on family farms, so I know how to do most any kind of farm work. If it is a lady I am asking, which quite frankly seems to be the case more than half the time, I offer to help them if they are doing something outside. If it is a woman you are talking to, be particularly respectful and keep an appropriate social distance. I never want to make anyone uncomfortable. I really prefer talking to a woman rather than a man—seems to work for me more often. Don't ask me why! Never go to someone's home to ask permission to hunt looking like a slob, or with beer/liquor on your breath or beer cans rattling in your truck—not smart! Quite frankly, I would not have dip in my mouth or cigarettes in my hand or my pocket. Remember that you never get a second chance to make a first impression. My hunting buddies will tell you that I have good success getting permission to hunt on private land. They say I am lucky. I don't think so! I think it is good manners and attention to detail that helps to make a positive impression on people, and that helps me get permission to hunt. I genuinely like country people because that is my own background. I enjoy visiting with them whether I get permission to hunt or not.

If I secure permission to hunt on a place, I make it a point to visit a bit with owners from time to time, not to the extent that I annoy them, but to establish a friendship that will last. I enjoy making friends as much or more than the hunting. I also never assume that permission to hunt one season means that I have permission to hunt forever. I seek permission for each coming season. I generally remain in contact with land owners and do things like send them a Christmas card or take a small gift when I visit them. After I know them, it is not too hard to think of some small gift that is appropriate. I personally tend to buy something for the lady of the house based on what I see in the house. I think that, if the lady of the house wants you to have permission to hunt, you are going to have permission to hunt—it does not always work the other way around. Quite often, landowners who have come to know and trust me will help me secure permission to hunt on neighboring properties. I've had some dial up a neighbor to ask permission for me to hunt with me standing there. To me, it is not just about the turkey hunting. I have made some wonderful friends as a consequence of my turkey hunting journeys; some are like family now, and I would go visit with them whether I hunted or not.

HUNTING CLUBS

Joining an existing hunting clubs is another option for private land access. Referrals are probably the most common means for clubs to acquire members, so you might be able to get in a club through a friend or acquaintance. The good thing about getting into a club this way is that you are likely to have better information about the club before joining—like how many people turkey hunt the land and how many acres the club encompasses (without exaggeration). Most hunting clubs in the south and mid-west are organized for deer hunting, and sometimes there are few if any turkey hunters in a club. They often welcome someone who is more interested in the turkey hunting than competing with them for deer. Clubs advertise in local news papers, in hunting magazines, local sales papers/bulletins, at local sporting goods stores, feed stores, church bulletin boards, and more. They even advertise on the Web, often on hunting forums and the likes. Be careful about getting into a hunting club. It can be a bad experience just as easily as it can be a good experience. Sometimes there are already turkey hunters in the club, there are limited "prime" areas for turkeys, and the other hunters know these areas and hunt them hard. This is not an ideal situation, and it can lead to frustration and/or conflict. Find out about the number of turkey hunters in the club and visit and explore the land to learn how much "good" turkey habitat can be found on the land.

Much of the time getting into a hunting club to turkey hunt either turns out great or it stinks. Sometimes all the club is looking for is someone to help pay the lease and they care absolutely nothing about your success in hunting on the lease. Be sure to find out the rules about guests, who hunts where and how that is decided, etc. Written rules are a plus—that way you know existing members don't just make them up as they go to suit themselves. Maps of the property and liability insurance are also a plus. Rules, maps, liability insurance, and such show organization, and that is generally a positive thing for a hunting club. Clubs that are just a loose confederation of "good ole boys," are not my preference for a hunting club. If you go to the club, and find beer cans and whisky bottles all over the land, around the camp, etc., that's not a good sign. I won't hunt around people who drink and hunt. Dangerous combination! I also dislike litter and the people who do it. Do your homework. If the hunting club dues are very reasonable, and you have other places to hunt, it may not be that big a deal if it does not work out well—you are not out much. If it is expensive, it is your only place to hunt, and it turns out badly, then it can ruin a turkey season. That's bad. Long story short, be cautious about joining a hunting club. It can work out great, but it can also be a bummer.

LEASING LAND

Leasing land can be expensive, but it is generally cheaper than owning it. If you can afford it, or you and a buddy or two partner-up to lease a place to turkey hunt, it can be a good way to get private land to hunt without actually buying it. Sometimes it will be advertised for lease, and sometimes you can simply approach an owner about leasing land. It is good to do your homework and know something about the land and the owner in advance. It is good to know the owner's name, how many acres they have, etc. You can get some of that information at a county courthouse (acreage, boundaries, etc.) since it is public information. Google Maps can allow you to get a "bird's eye view" of the property. It is also good to know something about the going price of leased land in the area. You want to offer the owner a fair price, but you don't want to pay more than necessary. If you do lease land, be sure you have a good legal contract specifying the terms of the lease. I prefer a one year lease initially, and then, depending on how it works out, a longer term lease might be appropriate. You can download standard lease documents from places like USLegalForms.com the Web—on this site they are not free, but are very reasonable and are tailored to different states. If you are leasing land with friends, you better make sure you have rules. If you are leasing it alone, that won't be a worry. If you partner with others, make sure you clarify in writing the rules about things like guests and coordination of hunting (who hunts what location and when) so you don't interfere with each other—two people cannot normally hunt the same exact spot. It has been my experience that issues pertaining to guests in particular have caused conflict more than any other thing in what I will call partnership leases. It is a good idea to purchase liability insurance. The National Rifle Association and the National Wild Turkey Federation can help you secure such insurance and at reasonable rates. Talking through all these issues with proposed partners for such an endeavor can help to prevent future conflict. If you cannot agree on things up front, then don't do it. Going in on a lease with someone is kind of like getting married—you better be sure it is the right decision up front. You will find out what your partner is really like later!

PUBLIC LAND

In some states, there are many good public hunting alternatives available to turkey hunters. In other states, the opportunities are few. For instance, Arkansas, Kansas, and Mississippi have vast areas of public land for hunting. In other states like Florida or Texas the situation is quite different. Arkansas has millions of acres of National Forest land, and many management areas as well. Mississippi has many management areas, but less National Forest land. Kansas has lots of small management areas, and a few larger ones, some BLM (Bureau of Land Management Land), CRP land, and many, many "walk-in" turkey hunting areas. The walk-in areas are private land under contract with the state to provide turkey hunting access to hunters. They do the same for deer hunting and pheasant hunting. Nebraska and other Midwestern states have similar programs.

In my opinion, Kansas does the best job of any state I hunt in providing information to hunters that can help them find land to hunt, and even help assess its hunting potential. Kansas publishes a great hunting atlas, available from the Kansas Department of Parks and Recreation. That atlas has maps, hunting statistics, etc. It is a great resource for planning a hunt on public or private land.

Texas has lots of turkeys but little public land, particularly west Texas. If you want to hunt Rios in Texas, you will generally have to hunt private land—either you know someone, or you pay! In Florida, there are quite a few management areas, but not too many from Orlando down where one finds the highly prized Osceola turkey (part of the coveted grand slam). The public land down there is really packed with hunters, particularly early in the season. I have turkey hunting buddies who have hunted quite a bit on public land in Florida. They say that the turkeys are there, but so are scores of hunters and that makes the hunting tough.

Hunting magazines are a good source of information about turkey hunting opportunities in various states. In the months prior to spring turkey season, some magazines do regional issues with good information on states to hunt, locations to hunt within the states, basic statistics on turkey populations, the hunting outlook, etc. Outdoor Life did this at one time, but I am not certain that they still do it. Other magazines do the same thing. Magazines tailored to specific states like the "Georgia Sportsman Magazine," do something similar for public hunting areas around the state.

Finding public ground to hunt is really easier than securing permission to hunt private land, but you generally share access with many more hunters. That means birds will be smarter and harder to hunt, the danger is greater (I don't like the idea of getting shot), and you may end up putting up with people who never heard of hunter ethics. To find public land, you can contact the game and fish or parks and recreation departments for the states of interest and request that they send you material in the mail. For most of that material, there is no charge. Some states give you very little and even require that you pay for maps. Brochures explaining regulations are generally free. Sometimes, you can get nearly anything you need from the appropriate department's website.

My preferred place for information about public hunting land is the Internet. If I am interested in a region, state, or specific area, I turn to the Web. I usually do key word searches for areas of interest using search phrases like "turkey hunting the Ozarks," or "public hunting Nebraska turkeys," and I use various combinations of these words for key word searches in Google, Bing, or whatever search engine. I refine my searches until I find what I seek. I normally read about hunting areas first on the official state website, be it the website of parks and recreation, game and fish, or whatever. They usually have links to information about various hunting areas, maps of areas, etc. Some have interactive state maps including all the management areas, allowing you to click your way the map accessing more detail about the areas. When I have found areas that I think I would like to hunt, having considered things like how many birds I can take, license fees, license requirements, season dates, etc., then I do key word searches on the specific areas I am considering and look for comments from other turkey hunters about hunting those areas. They are not always factual and useful, but I generally find the information helpful—most hunters only lie about their success or reasons for a lack thereof! Blogs and hunting forums abound with such information. It is also nice to know someone personally who hunts the area or areas to get first-hand information from a trusted source. I actually met my hunting buddy Tim as a result of our correspondence on a hunting forum prior to a hunting trip I had planned to the Black Hills years ago. I was looking for information and posted a question on a hunting forum to which he responded. I got his cell phone number and we met face to face weeks later in the Black Hills of South Dakota for just a few minutes. He put me on turkeys! He was about to head home to Louisiana. As it turned out, Tim hunted an area of Mississippi near where I grew up. We started hunting together the next year, became good friends, and have been hunting together ever since. I don't necessarily recommend you look for hunting companions on the Web, but I thought this story was worth throwing out for you. From information posted by individual hunters, I have decided to hunt, or not to hunt specific public areas. The Web is a great resource for finding information. I even use Google Earth to scout areas before I hunt them.

While I have killed a lot of turkeys on public ground, I prefer private land. I already noted the obvious differences in hunting pressure and safety concerns. I simply do not like hunting turkey in close proximity to other people. If I can hear a gobbler, I would like to be able to go to him and try to kill him. On public land, depending on the hunting pressure, if you hear a gobbler, you are quite likely not the only one who did. When multiple people move in on a bird, it is not a good situation. I find it very frustrating when I make a mistake and bust (scare off) a turkey. It is even more frustrating to me when someone else scares him off for me. This happened to me on 3 of 4 hunts on a piece of public ground in Nebraska last season—same fool messed me up all three times. While that can happen on private land, on most private land I hunt, I know if anyone else is hunting, and we usually coordinate our hunting so we don't interfere with each other. Turkey hunting is not like deer hunting. Many people don't really understand that—you don't want to hunt in one hollow and have someone in the next hollow some 200 or 300 yards away. While that works for deer hunting, it is not ideal for turkey hunting. You need a lot of room, so if you have to move on a gobbling turkey you can do so, or if you need to move looking for birds, you do that as well.

If you do opt to hunt public land, do your homework and find a place with a good turkey population and preferably without a lot of hunting pressure. I find that most, but not all, public land hunters will not venture far from roads and parking areas. If you are willing to walk for an hour or so to get to a place to hunt, you can often find yourself alone with the turkeys—that's ideal. I have a preference for areas that do not allow 4 wheelers because it means that it is less likely you are going to walk an hour to reach a secluded area, only to hear the "putt putt putt" of a 4 wheeler at day break. Not good! Look at maps of the area to make sure that when you walk a long way to avoid hunters, you don't unintentionally end up walking into an easily accessible area. It can happen—I've done it! I personally think it is wise, particularly if you are planning a hunting trip to a distant location, to plan your hunt a little later in the season. Often public areas that are quite crowded in the first two or three weeks of the season are almost empty in late season. The downside of hunting later in the season is that you will be hunting turkeys that are smarter and often call shy. The dumb ones are usually dead, so there are fewer turkeys to hunt as well. I have had good success with this strategy. I would rather hunt smart, call shy birds with no hunters around. The birds that remain are quite often older, wiser birds, and that means good spurs—I like that!

CHAPTER 7
TURKEYS AND TURKEY BEHAVIOR

I will start this section with a short description of the turkey, based largely on age and sex, so that terminology used throughout the book will be clear. I will explain as well how to identify turkeys up close and at a distance. I will also address the behavior of turkeys, particularly as it relates to the breeding season.

Spring season is about hunting gobblers, so I will start by describing gobblers. I will describe gobblers of different ages, then hens in essentially the same way. Since it is illegal to kill a hen during spring season, and in some states jakes are off limits, proper identification is important. Moreover, if you see a bird at a distance, it helps to know whether it is a hen or gobbler, jake or mature gobbler, before spending the time to cover that distance to hunt the bird.

GOBBLERS IN GENERAL

Generally, gobblers are bigger than hens and darker. They generally look almost black at a distance, especially from the front, but up close one will observe that they have red, bronze, purple, and green on the tips of their feathers. The sun really brings the colors out. From the back, they will appear more bronze colored, but generally look darker than hens. Gobblers tend to be broader across the back than hens, and they have beards and spurs, which hens typically do not. The head is blue, red and white. Mature gobblers have a white skull cap on the top of their heads—looks like a white beanie cap. It tends to grow thicker with age and is more prominent on older birds, especially during breeding season when you see them displaying. There have been times when that white skull cap was the first thing I spotted of a gobbler coming through the woods. Gobblers have wattles on their necks and bumps that resemble small warts (caruncles) on the upper neck and head. Wattles are comprised of fleshy, bubbly looking tissue around the upper portion of the neck and they are red, pink, white and blue. The head and upper neck of gobblers thus has few feathers. The color of the head and neck can change very quickly when a gobbler becomes excited—blood flow increases as does the intensity of the blue and red coloring—the red becomes a bright, blood red. Gobblers have snoods (I call it a goozle) right above their beaks. Hens have them too, but theirs are very short and a gobbler's is quite long, hanging down past his beak when he is excited. It is my observation that the neck feathers of Merriam gobblers tend to extend further up their necks during the early spring turkey season, probably because the ones I hunt live in areas where winter is very harsh, and the feathers are needed for warmth in winter.

Gobblers tend to have longer legs than hens, and tend to walk more upright than hens. The upright posture, generally larger size, and darker color can help one distinguish gobblers from hens at long distances. If they happen to be strutting, it makes it even easier to ID gobblers.

Gobblers have beards that protrude from the upper, middle of the chest. They are actually feathers but look like coarse hairs—kind of like an ugly, coarse, ponytail sticking out of the gobbler's chest. While some turkey hunters like to brag about beard length, the beard does not tell you much about the age of a bird. A 2 year old gobbler can have a thicker, longer beard than a mature 5 year old gobbler. The spurs are the best indicator of a gobbler's age. Spurs resemble a spike and protrude from the rear of the lower legs—the scaly, boney part of the leg. Spurs are battle weapons that gobblers use to inflict sometimes serious wounds on each other when fighting to establish dominance. I have killed numerous gobblers with spur wounds in their chest area. Spurs are bone covered with a horny tissue and can grow to be slightly over two inches. I have heard people talk about spurs longer than 2 inches, but I have personally never seen any that long. A gobbler with spurs exceeding 1 ½ inches is an exceptional trophy. Spurs often tend to turn up as they get longer, hence the name "limb hanger." A limb hanger is a gobbler you can hang from a limb by his curved hooks.

Mature gobblers: one relaxed and one strutting. Note the head coloration and decorations (white skull cap, wattles and snood).

JAKES

Jakes are birds of the year, born the previous spring. Jakes have beards that range from barely visible to 5 or 6 inches long—bigger ones we call "super" jakes. The beards of jakes tend to stick straight out rather than hang down. The spurs of jakes range from little nubs, to perhaps 3/8 inch in length. Jakes are generally smaller, thinner, and weigh less than older gobblers, but they are taller and leggier than hens. The heads and necks of jakes look different than that of more mature male turkeys. The head of a relaxed jake has more red coloration, and has less of the blue and white color or wattle found on more mature gobblers. Actually, the head of a jake has some of the characteristics of a gobbler head and some of the characteristics of a hen head. Jakes look a little like young boys in their early teens—tall, slight of build, and leggy. The gobble of a jake tends to be somewhat abbreviated as compared to a mature bird's gobble. They often yelp in the spring and their scratchy, coarse yelping with intermittent gobbling can sound pretty rough. Jakes are generally pretty dumb because they are young and inexperienced, but occasionally a jake can make a fool out of you just like a mature gobbler can.

Jake: slight of build and leggy, the beard is quite short, decorations about the head and neck area are less well developed, and generally no spurs are visible—spurs typically are just bumps.

TWO YEAR OLDS

During their second year of life, gobblers start looking and acting more like mature gobblers, but tend to lack the wisdom and caution of older birds. I think most experienced turkey hunters would agree that two year old gobblers tend to be easier to kill than more mature gobblers. Two year olds may do some of the same things dumb jakes do. Their beards tend to start hanging down their chest, but do not typically swing back and forth like the beards of more mature birds. Beard length is usually 7 inches or better. The spurs of two year old birds are generally going to be from ½ inch to ¾ inches in length, perhaps even a bit longer depending on genetics and nutrition. When they are not intimidated by mature gobblers in an area, two year olds love to gobble and can be much fun to work in the spring season. Two year olds generally come to the call more readily than mature gobblers and are more apt to respond to aggressive calling than mature birds.

MATURE GOBBLERS

Mature gobblers are birds 3 or more years old. Their spurs tend to be around an inch or longer. Beard length does not necessarily indicate age, but a mature bird will usually have a fairly good beard. Easterns where I hunt generally have thicker beards than the Merriams and Rios in places I hunt them. Mature birds are often called "swinging beards" in the south because their beards are generally relatively long and heavy, and literally swing back and forth as the birds walk and feed. Spurs are a more reliable indicator of age than beard length. My rule of thumb is ½ to ¾ inch spurs for 2 year old birds, 7/8 to 1 1/8 inches for 3 year olds, 1 ¼ inches for 4 year olds, and approaching 1 ½ inches for birds 5 years old and older. Note that there are exceptions. Spur length like beard length depends on nutrition and genetics, just like beard characteristics and overall body size. Merriam gobblers in the Black Hills of South Dakota tend not to grow long spurs as rapidly as birds in the south and lower Midwest, probably due to the harsh winter conditions and lack of agricultural crops to eat. Up there, a 4 or 5 year old gobbler may have only 1 inch, to 1 and 1/8 inch spurs, and their beards tend to be somewhat spindly compared to Eastern gobbler beards. The breast of mature gobblers tends to kind of waddle from side to side when they walk, and they are typically quite wide across the back. A mature eastern may weigh in excess of 20 pounds, Rios typically around 18, and Merriams around 16 pounds in mountainous areas, and a bit more in areas with agriculture. Mature birds, especially when hard hunted, tend to be wiser and harder to kill. A bird with spurs 1 ¼ inches or better is a good bird in nearly anyone's book because calling one to the gun is a challenge. A heavy bird does not necessarily mean an old bird. They tend to drop off as they get older, thus weigh less. They tend also to weigh less at the end of breeding season than at the beginning because sex trumps sustenance during the heavy breeding period. My buddy Ed killed what I think may be the oldest bird I ever called to the gun. He weighed only 14 pounds, was somewhat frail, but had very straight 1 ½ inch spurs. That gobbler now adorns Ed's den wall.

HENS IN GENERAL

Hens tend to be chestnut colored, have feathers extending further up the neck, possess less distinctive wattle on their necks, and they are smaller than gobblers. Their heads tend to be a blue gray. As far as size, hens are generally half to three-fourths the size of gobblers. Hens generally carry themselves a bit differently than gobblers, tending not to walk quite so erect but instead hunched over forward a bit. When alert or excited, they will tend to stand more erect like a gobbler. A mature hen will tend to have a raspier, coarser yelp than young hens, and older hens tend to have more wattle than younger hens. The wattle on even an old hen is still not enough to be noticed much. I have observed more wattle on dominant hens among my pen raised wild turkeys. Perhaps it is related to hormones. I don't profess to know for sure. Among a flock of hens, there is a pecking order just as there is with chickens. An old boss hen usually more or less runs the show, even with a gobbler in the flock. She will usually dictate the direction and timing of flock movement, not the gobbler. He is just along for the ride!

Hens with gobbler: This appears to be a scrawny two year old gobbler, but even he is noticeably larger than the two hens in front. The sun shining on their backs make the lighter coloration of hens less obvious in this picture.

YOUNG HENS

Young hens tend to look very little different from older hens, other than being smaller in size and thinner. I have observed that they also tend to have even less wattle than older hens. The yelp of a young hen is generally higher pitched than the yelp of an older hen, but that is not always true. Young hens are generally followers and go where the older hens lead them. Gobblers breed hens in their first year. Hens tend to flock with family members, and young hens sometimes even lay eggs in the same nest as their mother.

BEARDED HENS

While hens generally do not have beards, that is not always the case. I have seen numerous bearded hens, young and old. Approximately 1 in a thousand hens will have a beard. I have killed bearded hens where legal, but don't care to do so anymore. In some states it is illegal to kill a hen, regardless, so it is important to be able to tell a hen from a gobbler. To me, size, color, head characteristics, and posture are key in identification. I usually don't have to see a beard to know whether I am looking at a hen or a gobbler. This ability to tell them apart improves with experience—the more you see, the more it helps!

Bearded hen: note the lack of color and decoration found on a gobbler's head. This one was a legal kill, but definitely a hen.

NOTEWORTHY DIFFERENCES IN THE SUBSPECIES

I have noticed some differences among the sub-species of turkeys I hunt that I think are worth noting. Merriam gobblers and hens in cold country like the Rockies and in the Black Hills, tend to look much more alike than gobblers and hens of other sub-species. The feathers run further up the necks of gobblers. Merriam gobblers and hens are both very dark as well, so that adds to the difficulty of positive identification. I hesitated to shoot at gobblers several times because I just was not sure whether I was looking at a gobbler or a hen. When a Merriam gobbler is not excited and the head engorged with blood and/or the bird strutting, he does not look very much different from a hen. Of course, if they gobble that is all you need to know. It is a gobbler! When I see Merriam hens and gobblers together, the generally larger size of the gobbler makes positive ID a bit easier.

Rio gobblers in areas I hunt seem to have a little paler colored heads than eastern gobblers. Their heads look a little more pinkish colored (if there is such a color) to me than eastern or Merriam gobblers, however the big old head of a Rio gobbler is not easily confused with the head of a Rio hen—they tend to look quite different. In most places where I hunt Rios, the terrain is open (croplands), and I typically have a visual on a bird or birds for a fairly long period of time. That generally makes it easier to ID gobblers and even to distinguish the more mature birds from other gobblers. This brings to mind something else I find noteworthy about Rios. Rio gobblers tend more often to hang together than Merriam and Eastern gobblers. I have on many occasions seen flocks with 3 to 10 mature Rio gobblers during the peak of breeding season, and even more in west Texas. I find that behavior to be quite rare among the Merriam and Eastern gobblers in areas where I hunt. Note that I said where I hunt. I am not suggesting that this is always the case!

Gobbler feet are generally larger than those of a hen, and thus they make a heavier impression in the ground—deeper, more distinctive track. I will have more to say about tracks in the chapter on scouting for turkeys. I feel that I should point out that just because a bird struts, that does not mean it is a gobbler. I had an old boss hen that strutted exactly like a gobbler. If a bird struts odds are it is a gobbler, but like a turkey having a beard, it is not proof positive of the sex of a turkey.

THE MATING SEASON

This is a primer on the stages of the mating season. How you hunt, how you call, best times for hunting, etc., should take the stage of the breeding season into consideration. I will divide the mating season into 4 stages. Other people may describe it differently. This is based largely on my experience hunting birds, and what I have read about turkeys in scholarly journals—scientific studies by wildlife researchers—and not so much what I read in hunting magazines.

Stage I starts with the gobblers feeling that urge to breed and demonstrating mating behavior. Gobblers start to seek out and establish a territory, particularly the mature birds. They start feeling their oats and gobbling, displaying, fighting among themselves, etc. Bachelor groups start to break up as the gobblers prefer the company of hens to other gobblers. It's the start of breeding season, and comparable to pre-rut for whitetail bucks. Early in stage I the hens are not quite ready to breed and pretty much ignore the gobblers' advances. Early in this stage, gobblers will typically be gobbling their heads off in the early morning. It is during this stage that they are easier to call to the gun than in any other stage of the breeding season. Note that I did not say easy; I said easier! Some are never easy to call, but during this stage when they are horny and the hens are ignoring them, they generally respond well to the call. In some states, the turkey season start dates correspond reasonably well to this stage and the season may open in time for you to get after your gobbler during the first peak of gobbling that starts in stage one and continues into stage II. This is a good time to call a gobbler to the gun. In some years I have called gobbler, after gobbler, after gobbler during this magic time. All too often it was right before season, so all I could do was take pictures and enjoy the show. Hens start to become receptive to gobblers advances as Stage I progresses, then begins Stage II.

Stage II is when the hens are ready to breed and the breeding starts in earnest. Gobblers are likely still gobbling their heads off on the roost; however, after they leave the roost, they don't gobble as much. Early in Stage II gobblers are still assembling their harem—inviting hens to join them. They will gobble some on the ground as the morning progresses, and intermittently throughout the day. Because they have hens with them almost from the very moment their feet hit the ground in the morning, they can be a bit more challenging to call. It is in this stage that they start to become "henned up." That simply means that, having started a harem, they are with hens most of the day. During this stage, gobblers are breeding the hens intermittently from daylight to dark. The hens tend to stay with the gobblers and other hens (the harem) pretty much from fly down to fly up. This is one of the most difficult times to kill a gobbler. Why would he leave the harem in the hand, for the proverbial "bird in the bush?" I have killed gobblers in stage II by getting very close to them on the roost, getting them on their way back to roost in the evening, and by calling the hens. Sometimes, if you can get an old boss hen to respond to aggressive calling, she will bring her gobbler right to you. In an area with plenty of turkeys, there will almost always be satellite birds that don't get the girls. These are often 2 year old birds, and they may respond readily to the call if you can find them. It is not unusual to find 2 or more of those 2 year olds running together just as the Jakes tend to do. In the case of Rios, bachelor groups comprised of jakes and 2 year olds are not uncommon.

Stage III is when the gobblers are still henned up, but the hens are starting to lay eggs. They are not setting (incubating the eggs) yet, just slipping away to lay an egg every day or two. As the season progresses they seem to leave a little earlier each day. Also, more and more of the hens start doing this. Early in stage III hens may go lay and return to the gobbler, but as the stage progresses, they seem to leave later in the day and are less inclined to return to the gobbler. It seems to me that later in stage III hens prefer to feed around by themselves and with other hens, often not too far from their nest site. They may still roost with or in close proximity to gobblers in stage III. As this stage progresses, the likelihood of catching a gobbler by himself later in the day increases. I have killed many gobblers in the afternoon and late morning during stage III. If you can get a gobbler to respond to your call more than once, you have a pretty good chance of killing him. Moving around an area and prospect calling tends to be effective in Stage III, and afternoon hunting has been quite productive for me in stage III.

Stage IV is the final stage of the season. During this stage, most of the hens are setting and the odds of catching a gobbler by himself or with other gobblers, even on the roost, are pretty good. Gobblers start to hang out together more in this stage. You might see 2 or more gobblers together with no hens during this stage, or see gobblers by themselves. One would often find Rios in groups, whereas Eastern and Merriam gobblers, at least in places I have hunted, seem to prefer solitude, or at least very few gobbler friends for company. Gobblers may be roaming again as they search for a hen. Fewer hens will be spotted because they are setting on their nests. That does not mean you will see no hens and nothing but gobblers; remember these stages represent generalizations about turkey mating season behavior. Some hens won't set for one reason or another and they will be around and even setting hens leave the nest for short periods of time. The end of stage III and start of stage IV marks the second peak of gobbling activity. Gobblers are lonely again and tend to gobble more often, in hopes of locating hens. I think they tend to gobble best in the mornings but not quite like they did at the beginning of the breeding season—seems to me to be almost habit for them at this point to gobble, since they have been doing it all season, but they are getting worn down. This is a good time to kill a gobbler as their sex drive and the lack of hens makes them vulnerable again. Toward the end of stage IV, the breeding is done and you may encounter gobblers that have no interest what-so-ever in your calling. We say, they are "done" at this point. I have killed a lot of gobblers in Stage IV, some in the mornings, but probably more in the afternoon. Sometimes in stage IV, the only way you can kill a gobbler is to ambush him. It is not my preferred means of taking a gobbler, but I have done it when a gobbler simply would not work (respond to calling). This is when woodsmanship and general hunting skills are particularly important ingredients in success. Some states close their seasons before the turkeys reach stage IV of the breeding season.

CHAPTER 8
SCOUTING

The basic approach to finding gobblers is essentially the same on private or public land. On private land, you can sometimes get good information from the owners about where they see turkeys, where they hear turkeys, and more. If the owner is a farmer who lives on the property, or frequents the property to feed cows, etc., he/she is going to be a good source of information about where the turkeys are located. Take the time to talk with them and learn what you can from them. They can sometimes tell you where they see or hear them at different times of day, where they have seen gobblers, if they have seen the gobblers by themselves and where they have seen them, about any particularly large gobbler or gobblers they have seen, and that can be very helpful information in formulating a good strategy to take a gobbler on the place. If you secured permission early in the year, it does not hurt to visit the owner close to the start of the season. Most farmers I know like to talk, but I make sure I don't interfere with them getting their work done.

If hunting on a club/lease, other members can sometimes tell you where they have heard and/or seen birds, especially gobblers. If they are turkey hunters too, you typically won't get much out of them. They see you as competition. I do find that older turkey hunters tend to be more helpful than younger turkey hunters. I think the older hunters have figured out that it is not just about killing turkeys and they enjoy seeing other turkey hunters be successful. I will say more about that later. "Big time" deer hunters on the other hand are generally much more inclined to help you out, especially if you are primarily a turkey hunter, and they don't see you as competition for deer. You may think I am kidding, but I am serious about my characterization of the two groups of hunters and their willingness to help you find turkeys on club land. Note that where turkeys are in the fall and early winter during deer season is not necessarily where they will be in the spring; however, just knowing that turkeys, and gobblers in particular, are in the area is helpful. Years ago, I watched 7 gobblers from my deer stand in December while deer hunting. I killed two of them on opening day of turkey season around 300 yards from that stand—one at daylight and one at noon. I know for sure that one was with that bunch because he had a very distinctive beard—like a boat paddle. I still have the beard! My point is that they might not be in the same spot, but can be in the same general area. It depends a lot on the food source they are using.

On public land, area wildlife managers can give you some of the same type of information as private land owners, but normally they are just going to tell you what areas hold good numbers of turkeys. Some good information can be obtained from folks living in such areas if you are actually visiting the areas scouting for turkeys. In the Black Hills, we often get good information from the locals when eating breakfast at local restaurants. For whatever reason, it seems that not many of them turkey hunt, and they are more than willing share information about where they see turkeys. Recognize that unless they have seen them lately, they may not be there anymore! Current sightings are the most helpful, and it helps if the sightings were in areas you can hunt, or at least in close proximity to those areas.

In spring, gobblers are going to be where the hens are and that is generally near good nesting areas. What exactly is good nesting area varies from one area of the country to the other, but nesting hens generally need food, cover, water, and open ground when the poults hatch. Hens like to nest where they have enough ground cover to hide their nest (brush and briars, tree tops, etc. and not so much just tall grass), and they like relatively safe areas where water and food are easily accessible from the nest site. It has been my experience that hens that find a good nesting site will tend to use it year after year; not necessarily the same nest, but the same area. In the south and Midwest, all the way up to the Dakotas, it seems that hens prefer fairly open country as opposed to heavy timber for nesting. Good edge—the convergence of eco zones—is ideal because the hens have dense cover for nesting and open ground for feeding and for moving about with their poults when they hatch. Early in the season, when the hens don't have nesting on their mind yet, just breeding, they may still be in heavily wooded areas where food is abundant—their late winter habitat. They can scratch for insects and the likes that can be found under leaves in hardwood forests in the south, and the same is true of woodlots in the Midwest. In the abundant Ponderosa pines found in the Black Hills of South Dakota and NW Nebraska, Merriam turkeys scratch up pine nuts and bugs, and eat lots of green vegetation. In west Texas, where there is much more natural food than one might think, Rios like mesquite seeds, grass seeds, bugs, small flowers, grasses and clovers. During the breeding season and even in the weeks leading up to the actual breeding, gobblers like to strut their stuff in areas where they can be seen, thus open areas attract them. In heavily wooded areas, even small open areas are attractive to turkeys and can become a gobbler's strut zone. New Clear-cuts are attractive to turkeys in the spring, but as they become thick with undergrowth—usually their 2nd year in the south, but may be 3rd of 4th year further north—turkeys seem inclined to avoid them. Hens may nest in the edges of them, but they don't like to wander through thick cover because it puts them at risk for becoming a meal for a coyote or similar predators.

To hunt gobblers, you need to know where they are actually located when you plan to hunt them. My preference is to know enough about a gobbler, that on the morning I intend to hunt, I can get to within 100 or 200 yards of him before he leaves the roost (fly-down). More than general information is necessary. More often than not, this involves legwork—getting out on the land and looking around for sign, looking for turkeys, and listening for gobblers.

In the hardwoods of the south, I spend most of my scouting time walking around in the woods looking for sign. I look for turkey scratching which is probably the easiest sign to find in hardwoods. Turkey scratching looks like chicken scratching if you have ever seen it. Scratching tends to be small plate size openings in the leaves that expose the dirt beneath along with the bugs and remaining mast; this is the food that turkeys seek. Leaves tend to be piled more at one end of the scratching, the end at which the turkey is standing when it scratches. If there are only a few turkeys working an area, there might not be large concentrations of such sign. You often find turkey scratching under oak and beech trees, next to the trunks quite often, and if it is very dry, you are apt to find it in moist areas like creek bottoms, river bottoms, etc. That is where the turkeys can find bugs. In the Midwest scratching can be found around corn fields, Milo (grain sorghum) fields, hay bales, and in woodlots between fields. In the Black Hills scratching can be found in aspen groves and in stands of Ponderosa pine (in the pine straw). If there are many birds in the flock, the area may look like someone took a garden tiller down through the woods. Generally speaking, the diameter hen scratching will be a bit smaller than that of a gobbler, and when you have seen enough of it, you can generally tell the difference between the two. Gobblers are bigger birds generally, and have longer legs; thus, their scratching tends to be a bit larger and typically a bit longer—size of a large platter and hen the size of a small plate. If I find larger scratching that is sparsely scattered (10 to 30 foot between each) through the woods moving in a particular direction, I generally assume it to be a gobbler. Quite a bit of it may mean more than one gobbler. You can tell the direction the birds are moving by the end of the scratching where the debris is piled. The most debris is at the opposite end of the direction the turkey is facing when it scratches—ends up under or behind the turkey as they scratch.

On the left are open hardwoods so common in the south. The hilltop on the right is typical of the Black Hills, where scratching can be found in the pine needles that Merriams search for pine nuts.

If scratching is fairly fresh and the ground is soft enough, you can look closely and see tracks in the scratching. Larger tracks tend to be gobbler tracks, and small tracks tend to be hen tracks. What I like to see is old scratching and new scratching, indicating that the birds are using the area pretty regular. In some areas where armadillos are common, they tear up the woods as well. They root stuff up like hogs, and their scratching tends to look like it was made by a drunkard that dragging a stick through the leaves—it zigzags all over the place. With experience, it is not hard to tell the difference between turkey sign and just about any other. With some experience you can usually tell, within a day or so, the age of scratching. If it rained a week ago, and the scratching has been rained on, you know it is not real fresh. If it looks pretty fresh and tracks in it are very distinctive such that you can see the scale pattern on the toes, it is probably very fresh. If you have any doubt, use your foot or hand to scratch out a spot next to it and compare the two. That can tell you if it is very fresh or not. If you scout an area frequently—it is good to do that—you can make a mental note of what you see each time and thus recognize anything new.

Old versus new: the scratching on the left has been rained on and has some debris in it to suggest that it is old. The dirt is freshly disturbed with the scratching on the right, so it is obviously fresh.

Scratching in different settings looks different: scratching in Nebraska cornfield on left and in Arkansas hardwoods on right.

Often in proximity to scratching you will find dusting areas, or dust bowls. They look a little like scratching, but are deeper and bigger. A well used dusting area can be quite large and comprised of numerous dust bowls. Much fresh dirt is exposed and often feathers are found in and around the dust bowls. As the name implies, they tend to be dusty—there is an abundance of loose, powdery dirt. You can tell the turkey put more effort into making a dust bowl than they do just scratching for food. Turkeys lay in those dust bowls and use their wings to spread dust throughout their feathers. It helps to rid themselves of parasites like mites and such. For turkeys, dusting is kind of like taking a bath. If you ever watch them do it, you will observe that they seem to really enjoy it. I have killed turkeys at well used dusting areas, but they are not a sure thing. If it looks like it is used frequently—many bowls, freshly used, fresh tracks and feathers—it is a better bet. I sometimes go sit near a dusting area when I have been unsuccessful in my early morning hunt. It seems to me that the turkeys like to hit the dusting areas late morning and in the afternoon when they are taking a break from feeding and are just looking for a place to pass the time and socialize a bit. During midday turkeys will dust themselves, preen (groom) themselves, and just lay around in the shade, particularly in warm weather. I don't recall having seen a mature gobbler dust, but in the spring, if dusting areas attract hens, gobblers will be close by.

Dust bowls in a food-plot. Note that turkeys had to put considerable effort into cleaning out this spot in the grass.

The tracks of turkeys are generally pretty easy to recognize. They are larger than crow tracks (some people mistake crow tracks for turkey tracks but crow tracks tend to be no more than 2 inches long), and turkey tracks are not so large as a blue heron tracks (generally found around ponds and will be in the water as well as on the bank). Gobbler and hen tracks tend most often to look somewhat different. Gobblers, because they tend to be larger than hens, have larger feet than the hens. With gobblers, the toes are thicker and longer, and a large gobbler track may be 4 to 5 inches from the heel to the tip of the middle toe. Hen tracks tend to be smaller, probably averaging 3 inches form heel to toe. Jake tracks will sometimes fool you, as they will look like large hen tracks. Studying the shape of tracks will help identify the likely source. The outside toes of hens tend to be a bit shorter in comparison to their middle toe than is the case for gobblers, where all three toes appear closer to the same length. I look for tracks in scratching if it is fresh, in roads, around water (ponds, mud puddles, sand bars), around fields, in snow, etc. Basically, I look for tracks anywhere the ground is soft enough for a turkey to make a track. The tracks can tell me if turkeys are in an area, how many are in an area, if gobblers are in an area, when turkeys use an area, direction of travel, etc. All of this is important information in formulating a strategy to hunt an area. Learning to read sign and understand what it tells you about turkey behavior is important to success and it takes time.

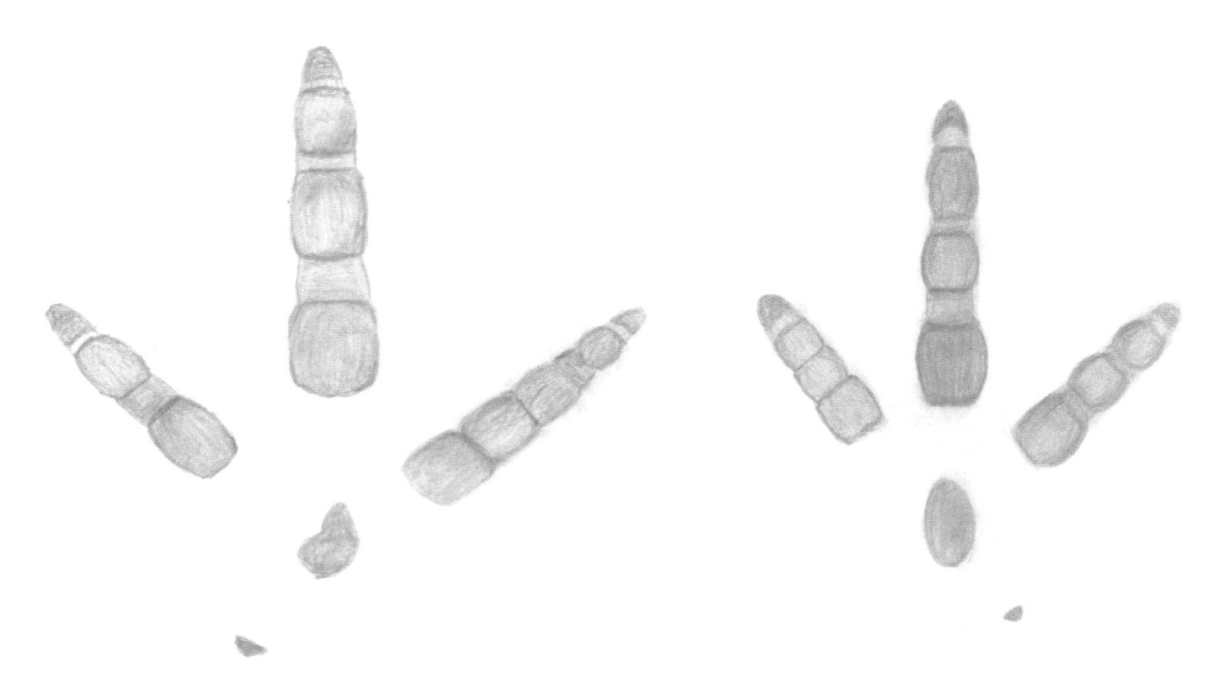

Gobbler track on left and hen track on right. Note the gobbler track is typically larger and note the relative size of middle and outer toes (closer to same length on gobbler foot). The toes seem generally to be more spread out in gobbler tracks. (Illustrations by Ottis Holland)

Turkey droppings don't look much like anything else—it should not be easy to confuse with coon droppings, deer droppings, etc. It tends most often to be fairly solid and is generally colored white and green or brown when fresh. The green and brown part may turn nearly black as it gets older and dries. When it gets really old, the color fades out of it leaving it very light colored. If it is real fresh, it will tend to still be moist on the outside. If it is sort of fresh—day or two—it will tend to be moist on the inside. That generalization varies from area to area. It is pretty much true in the southeast. In the Black Hills and in the upper Midwest, droppings generally dry out really fast due to low humidity, so determining how old droppings are is not so easy. If the turkeys are eating lots of green vegetation, the droppings may be just little quarter size globs of dark green/dark brown feces—kind of like a large Hershey's Kiss that melted.

Hen droppings and gobbler droppings are generally quite distinctive in their shape. Gobbler droppings tend to be long and J shaped. Very large j-shaped droppings (size of the tip of your little finger) tend to be from mature gobblers and smaller ones (smaller than a pencil) from jakes, but the basic shape is the same. Hen droppings tend to be more like an oblong glob (more egg shaped—not surprising considering where the eggs come from), or in a spiral shape. When scouting for gobblers to hunt, I am pleased when I find gobbler droppings and particularly pleased if some are old, some new, and some are in between. That shows regular use of an area by gobblers.

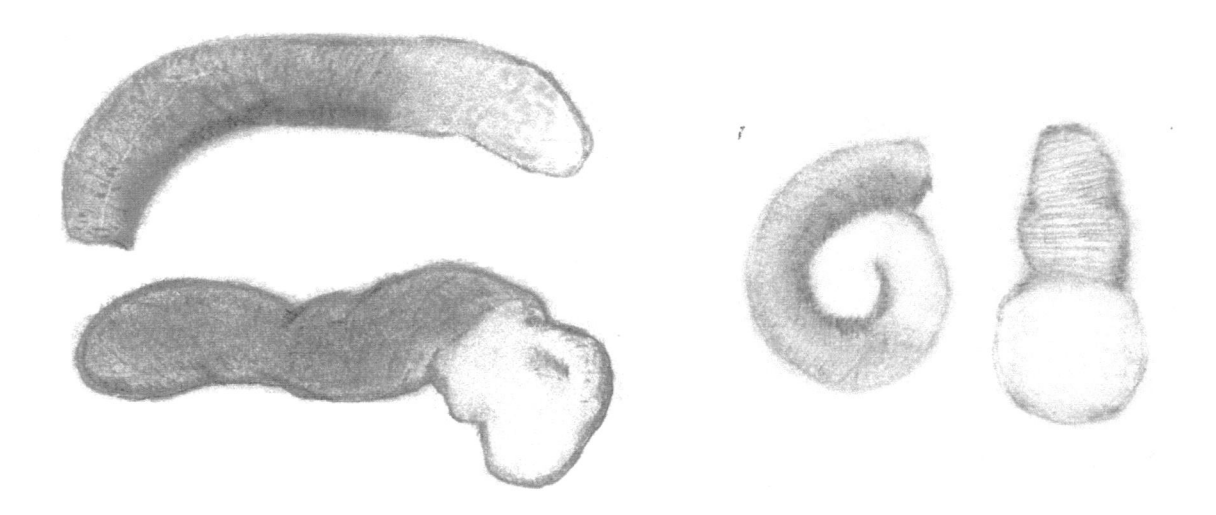

Gobbler droppings on the left and hen droppings on the right. (Illustrations by Ottis Holland)

In addition to observing various types of turkey sign in an area, I like to see the turkeys. If I have the luxury of time to scout an area, and there are large openings like fields around, I like to drive around or walk around with my binoculars and try to actually see gobblers. In the Midwest where I hunt, visual scouting is what I rely on most. As soon as I get to the area I plan to hunt, I take a drive around the hunting areas looking for gobblers out in fields. If it is hot, then the birds are not as likely to be out in the open areas in midday, but when it starts to cool a bit in the afternoon, say 4 o-clock or so, they tend to get back out in the fields and stay there until they start moving towards their roost area.

In the hardwood areas around the south where I hunt, I rely more on the physical sign of turkeys' presence and listening for gobblers in the mornings. Before season, I will go out very early, as if I were going hunting, and listen for gobblers around my hunting areas. The combination of physical sign (scratching, droppings, tracks, feathers, etc.), seeing turkeys, and hearing gobblers helps me decide where to hunt. In the Midwest, what turkeys I see and where I see them tends to be more important to me in deciding where to hunt.

Gobblers will sometimes gobble after they go up to roost in the evenings. It seems to me that they did it much more in the south some years ago than they do today. I am not sure why—maybe coyotes since we blame everything else on them! Roosting a gobbler—getting him to gobble after fly up—is worth a try, but don't expect regular success with this in the south. It gives you an advantage to know where the gobbler is when night falls because he will most likely be there in the morning. Knowing his exact location helps you to get close to him in the morning! When roosting a gobbler in the south, I try to be in the woods during the last hour of daylight, close to where I expect a gobbler to roost. I listen, not just for a gobble, but for wings beating as the bird or birds fly up. If the turkey doesn't gobble on the roost, then maybe I can hear him fly up. It helps! In the Midwest gobblers tend more readily to gobble from the roost in the evening. Merriam gobblers are very inclined to do so. I use a coyote call as a locator call all the way from Texas to South Dakota. It works very well. In the south to get a bird to gobble, it is best to hoot like an owl, a barred owl in particular. I use my mouth, and most anyone can learn to do so with practice, but one can also buy an owl hooter. Many companies make them. To mimic a coyote, use a coyote howler call. Merriam and Rio gobblers will readily gobble after flyup at the howling of a coyote.

Good scouting anywhere in the country should culminate with you knowing where to hunt a gobbler either in the morning or in the evening. I will have more to say about each in discussing calling and setups. With morning hunting, it is best if you can have the gobbler located in advance with good scouting. Ideally, you know where he is the evening before the morning of your hunt. Doing your homework with good scouting increases your odds of taking a mature gobbler. That is true whether or not you are hunting private or public land. On the morning of the hunt, if you arrive early like you should (before daybreak) and you get within a couple hundred yards of your gobbler, depending on the terrain and the situation, and he gobbles, you have at least increased your odds of making the kill.

If you have scouted really well and you set up in the exact right place, you have dramatically increased your odds of taking your bird. Being in that exact right spot is not that easy. Unless you have spent time scouting in the days before your hunt and observed the bird's movement (by sight, sound or both) after leaving the roost, or you know the area very well, your first hunt may turn out to be more a scouting expedition than hunting! Quite often I have eased in and got close to my bird only to have him fly down and leave with hens, or simply head off in the wrong direction. In short, I don't get my turkey. I try to learn from the situation then see if I can be better positioned the next day. If he heads off up a ridge other than the one you are on, flies into a field at a location other than your own, flies up to a bench above the one you are on, or whatever, pay close attention. It can help you fine tune your approach and be in a better position the next day. I have spent days patterning a bird before killing him, and have messed with old smart birds for weeks without ever killing them. You might think, not much of a turkey hunter! Well, if you turkey hunt long enough, you will encounter a bird like that—one you can chase all season and end up whipped in the end. Getting outsmarted by a critter with a brain the size of a pea will teach you humility.

CHAPTER 9
SETTING UP ON TURKEYS

How and where to best set up on a gobbler depends on the situation, but some general rules of thumb do apply. 1. You want to be close enough to your turkey for him to hear you, but not so close that you spook him. 2. You want to be hidden, but need an unobstructed view for shooting when the bird approaches. 3. You want to be able to get the shot when the bird comes within range, and preferably, you want him in range when you can see him. 4. You want to be safe. When I hunt on public land, safety is a big concern for me. I try to set up where I have a good chance of killing my turkey, but little chance of getting shot. I try as best I can to sit where I can see any approaching hunter, or any hunter who might be in the area when I arrive. I always want something behind me that protects me from behind, something like a large tree, rock, bluff or bank.

When deciding exactly where to sit, I try to envision which way the turkey might approach. The more you hunt turkeys, the more you understand their behavior, the more you will be able to "think like a turkey." That helps in anticipating the direction from which a gobbler might approach. You should remember that there will always gobblers that will surprise you by circling around you, or in some other way approaching from the "wrong direction." Some have a knack for coming from the worst possible direction. Sometimes a bird cannot come but one way because of obstacles around you like water or steep bluffs. Those obstacles can actually help you better predict the likely approach route, so learn how to use them in your favor.

For the actual setup, I like to pick a spot (tree, rock, etc.) that allows me to hide reasonably well, yet not restrict my movement or shot. I like the ground to be relatively flat, and if it is not, I use my boot to kick the dirt and rocks away to flatten it out some before sitting down—those turkey seats with adjustable legs come in handy in these situations. Sometimes it is necessary to use your hands a bit in this process. I rake away leaves and limbs that might make noise when I sit down. I basically clear out a spot large enough to sit quietly, but not so large that it attracts attention. Don't get too carried away because you want the area to look natural. Even with a padded seat, like the one on my turkey vest, a rock can become uncomfortable, so I try to get them out of the way. Remember, you may end up sitting for minutes or for hours so you want to be reasonably comfortable. If I am using one of my turkey seats with adjustable legs, all I really need to do is clear out the brush and leaves and adjust the legs to give me a flat place to sit. If the ground or the seat is not fairly level/flat, you tend to slide forward, backward, or sideways after sitting a while, and then you have to move to get back in good shooting position. Movement is a no-no when turkey hunting and in my opinion the cause of more spooked turkeys than any other single thing. I use my pruner to cut briars, limbs, vines, and saplings around me so I have a clear shot and clear path to move my gun around if necessary. If I am setting up by a tree and a gobbler's approach path is uncertain, I will usually clear out at least 180 degrees around the tree, so I can slide around it with ease if I must reposition myself as the turkey approaches from the opposite direction. Note: do not move if he is close!

When you actually sit down, you want to be facing the direction from which you expect the bird to approach. Get your gun up on your knee and pointed in the direction of the bird. As he gobbles and moves in your direction, keep the gun pointed in his direction, and ideally, in the most likely direction of approach. As you move your gun barrel to follow the gobbling of the bird, move very slowly—like cold molasses. You never know when a turkey or turkeys might approach silently, hen or gobbler, and their sharp eyes can detect even the slightest movement. There is nothing worse than to hear that sharp "putt…. putt…putt…putt." That sound is the alarm call for turkeys, and when you hear it, it usually means game over. If the turkey that is doing the putting is not the one gobbling and the gobbling bird hears it, he is quite likely to shut up and leave. The sound of an alarm putt carries further than you might think and turkeys are geared to hearing it and responding accordingly—it is a survival thing. If you were busted and the bird doing the putting leaves, don't assume the bird that was gobbling is gone. Wait a bit to see if he spooked, or if the hunt is still on. As long as the bird is gobbling and coming your way, keep your gun up and pointed in the direction of the bird until the moment of truth.

In open country like in Kansas, Texas, Nebraska, and Oklahoma, I sometimes set up in areas where there are no trees. Sometimes the only available cover is small mesquite trees, sage brush, buck brush, wheat, tall grass, etc. In this type terrain, you want to be concealed to the top of your head, so you need to set up in or against something fairly tall. I have ended up on my belly in grass, but I can tell you for sure, that is a last resort. It is uncomfortable, not to mention a bad shooting position. In rattlesnake country, it is DANGEROUS! In Kansas and Nebraska, plumb thickets are pretty common where I hunt. I often use my pruner to cut a hole in the edge of a plumb thicket and back up into it to set up. I can be well hidden, and have a good shot as well. I make sure I cut out enough of the surrounding cover to give me a good shot, but not so much that it makes it easy for a gobbler to spot me. I have done the same thing in buck brush, mesquite and sagebrush. My Gobbler Lounge is particularly handy for these setups because it is low to the ground, making it inconspicuous (camo material), and it is very comfortable because it gives me back support. I can sit comfortably for hours in that seat. I never knew I needed one until my buddy gave it to me for Christmas, but I will never be without one now. It is a little heavy so I don't carry it on all my hunts, but when I hunt in areas where I know it is likely needed, I throw it over my shoulder and carry it with me. In hunting open areas with few trees, selection of the right tree is pretty important. I like to select one that has a little brush around it to help break up my outline and hide me. Sitting next to a lone tree with nothing around it is about like sitting next to a fencepost and not a real good hide, but if it is my only choice, I might go with it.

It is also important to set up in a place that the gobbler will feel comfortable approaching. In the south where I hunt eastern gobblers, much of my hunting takes place in pretty heavy woods, most generally hardwoods. I find that turkeys in this part of the country generally prefer not to move through real thick cover. Passing through thick cover makes turkeys more vulnerable to predators, and I believe that is why they prefer to avoid it. In the west, particularly Texas and Oklahoma, I have seen Rios walk through thick brush I would never expect to see eastern gobblers use. I think one of the reasons for it is that they don't have much choice—to get from point A to point B, there may be no open route, so they have to move through thick cover. Rios seem to be accustomed to thick cover, and they use it. This is something to keep in mind; turkeys in different parts of the country tend to behave in ways consistent with survival in their world as it is! Tactics you use should reflect the turkey behavior where you hunt. In other words, don't expect Rios to act just like Easterns, or either to act just like Merriams. In some ways they are quite similar, but in significant ways they are different. It took me a while to figure that out! Furthermore, don't expect the same subspecies to act the same way in different environments. Turkeys must adapt to their surroundings to survive, and that means adjusting their behavior. If you hunt turkeys in different environments often enough, you will understand this well.

In open hardwoods I like to set up in a position where the gobbler will be in shooting range when he arrives at the position where the calling is coming from—my position! This usually means setting up with a small knoll, brushy area, blow-down, briar patch etc., in the expected line of approach. When the gobbler steps into view, I want him in range so that all I have to do is shoot. If a gobbler can see a long way, like a in a big hardwood hollow for instance, and can see where the hen should be but no hen is there, he will quite likely hang up (stop coming towards you). He might give you a good show by strutting and drumming, but will probably stay out of range—a frustrating situation indeed! Decoys can be helpful in such setups and that is why I generally have one in my vest; just in case I need it. If a gobbler can see a decoy or two where the sound is coming from, and he cannot see you, he might come on into gun range. This holds true for any kind of terrain in which a bird can see a long way—fields, meadows, prairie, underbrush-free mountain side, etc. Since open areas abound in the Midwest, I tend more often to use decoys there than in the timber country of Arkansas, Mississippi, and Georgia, where I hunt.

I have killed several gobblers from this, my favorite setup spot, on my property. When a gobbler is in sight, he is in range!

Unfortunately, turkeys all too often hang up because of water or other obstacles. I have seen gobblers refuse to cross a stream I could step across. On the other hand, I have called gobblers across big creeks and even beaver ponds, but don't count on it! Those instances were exceptions to the rule. A gobbler's response to an obstacle depends on just how bad he wants to come to your location—to the hen you pretend to be—and a host of other variables, most of which you don't control! Other obstacles that can cause a bird to hang up include: fences, particularly hog-wire fences which are pretty common in the south, gullies, ditches, roads, large openings, and very dense cover. Yes gobblers can fly, but more often than not, they won't do it to get over an obstacle. I am not sure that anyone but the turkeys know why they act that way! When scouting, make a mental note of possible obstacles and take them into consideration in planning your hunt and picking a setup. Try to set up where obstacles that might cause a turkey to hang up will not be between you and your gobbler. If that is not possible, like when you find yourself on the opposite side of the creek from your gobbler, and there is nowhere and/or no time to cross, try to sit close enough to the edge to shoot across it if he hangs up on the other side. I offer the same advice for dealing with fences, gullies and the likes.

Sometimes gobblers will hang up for other reasons. I have encountered smart old gobblers that were educated by other hunters, and they would come to within about 75 yards, then start drumming and strutting as they waited for the hen to come to them. That is what a real hen will normally do; she will go to the gobbler. A hunter cannot do that! This kind of hang-up (behavior) can become a pattern for these old birds. Sometimes you can team up on such birds; one hunter sits back 50 to 75 yards to do the calling while the other sets up in a forward position to take the shot—maybe with a decoy, maybe not. While this trick is not fool proof, it has worked for me and other turkey hunters I know.

CHAPTER 10
CALLING A TURKEY

Calling a turkey is as much art as science. Every gobbler is different and every situation is a little different, so knowing what exactly to say to get a gobbler to come to you is an educated guess! In other words, there is no sure thing. What works to bring one gobbler to the gun might spook another. What drives a 2 year old gobbler crazy might scare off an older, wiser bird. I am going to tell you in this section what I have learned about calling turkeys. I have learned it mostly from hunting turkeys, but also from other people who hunt turkeys, from listening to and observing turkeys I raised, and from things I have read over the years. Hopefully, there is something here for everyone, from the beginner to the experienced turkey hunter. The various types of calls were discussed in an early chapter of this book. This section focuses on the calling itself, but will occasionally address issues related to call choice and use. It is hard to talk about calling a turkey without talking some about the calls (devices and the sounds turkeys make).

You need to understand that the natural order of things is for the gobbler to gobble and the hens to go to him. You are, as the late Ben Lee put it, "trying to reverse nature," when you try to get the gobbler to come to you. Young gobblers, like Jakes (birds of the year) and 2 year olds, are more likely to come running to the call than smart old mature gobblers. Wise old birds (3 years old or more), especially those that have been hunted, are more inclined to expect hens to come to them. You should always keep that in mind. You need to be smart, cool under pressure, and patient, to fool the old boys into coming to your gun. Furthermore, you need to learn how and when to call and when not to call.

TURKEY VOCALIZATIONS

Turkeys make many sounds. I will define the basic sounds at this point because I will use the terms in discussing calling.

Mating yelp—series of soft seductive yelps made by a hen turkey in the spring—yelp…yelp…yelp…yelp….yelp. The mating yelp may be a series of as few as two (yelp, yelp), but more often 3 to 8. The hen may string yelps together in succession like yelp…yelp, yelp…yelp…yelp…yelp, yelp…yelp, pause, then yelp…yelp….yelp…. yelp…yelp…yelp, and she may yelp very little. During mating season, it is not unusual to hear a hen moving through the woods, yelping on occasion as she goes. Sometimes a hen will stay in one spot and yelp, getting a little louder, and a little louder, as she tries to get a gobbler to respond.

Aggressive yelp/excited yelp—a long, loud series of yelps that sound like scolding or pleading— often intermingled with excited cutting. Hens often make this call when scolding each other, or insisting that a gobbler "come on over here."

Assembly call—made by hens, most often to call her young poults to her. It consists of a long series of yelps that may increase a bit in intensity toward the end. It more or less says to the other turkeys, I'm over here so come find me!

Lost call—similar to the Assembly call, but consisting of more yelps and greater intensity at the end. It sometimes seems to go on and on until the hen runs out of breath. The lost call is often used by hunters in the fall. The fall hunter will attempt to locate and break up a flock, then use the lost call and perhaps the kee kee to entice turkeys to reassemble.

Kee Kee—a call made by young turkeys. It sounds almost like a whistle and is often combined with some high pitch yelping—the combination of kee kees and yelping is called the kee kee run. This call is made by young turkeys to keep in touch and locate each other when separated. Like the lost call, the kee kee is used mostly for fall hunting, but it can be used in spring as well.

Cluck—a soft, short, single note sound made by turkeys—cluck, cluck,......, cluck. It is often used by hens to keep in contact with other turkeys as they feed through woods or fields. It is turkey small talk. During mating season, hens often cluck intermittently with their mating yelps. When hunting, one should be careful not to cluck too sharply, as it might resemble the putt which is a warning call.

Putt—essentially a loud, hard cluck. Putts are often made in succession, with a second or few seconds between, as the bird paces back and forth assessing the danger. Putts can become more rapid and louder as a bird becomes certain there is cause for alarm and starts to move away. It is a warning call. Turkeys putt to warn other turkeys of danger. If you hear it when hunting, you probably messed up! Hens and gobblers both putt, but a gobbler's putt is usually louder, and more coarse.

Purr—kind of like the purr of a cat—purrrrr, purrrrr, purrrrr. It is a contented sound; kind of like the turkey is saying "life is good." This is a sound typically made by turkeys while they are dusting and/or feeding, thus I say that it is a sound associated with pleasure and contentment. The feeding purr is a little softer. I think the feeding purr helps turkeys to "stay in touch" as they move through the woods, and to share information about the discovery of food as they feed. A dusting bird's purrs seem to be a little louder as if to say, "this sure feels good."

Aggressive purr—much sharper and harder than the regular purr and signals aggression—don't mess with me. A dominant hen will often make this sound when scolding a strange hen that shows up on the scene.

Gobbler fighting purr—Like the aggressive purr of hens, only made by gobblers in challenging each other and when fighting. When combined with the wings popping as gobblers flog each other with their wings, fighting purrs create the very loud and unmistakable sound of a gobbler fight.

Cackle—rapid series of clucks strung together in a pretty long sequence. There are fly down and fly up cackles that turkeys, mostly hens, make as they fly to and from the roost. A mating cackle is a pleading cackle made by hens in conjunction with cutting and yelping in spring enticing a gobbler to "come on over here."

Cutting—rapid succession of sharp clucks often intermingled with aggressive/excited yelping. Cutting shows excitement or aggression.

Whine—as the name suggests it sounds like a long drawn-out cluck that generally increases a little in volume—often made in conjunction with a cluck or two. You can drag the lid across a **box call slowly to get an idea how it sounds.**

Gobble—a long drawn out goggle…gobble…gobble…gobble…gobble sound made by gobblers, primarily in mating season. It is used to attract hens and to say to other gobblers, I'm the man! Mature birds tend to have a long drawn out gobble and jakes tend to have a short abbreviated gobble. With jakes, gobbling may be mixed in with some rough sounding yelps. You cannot always judge the bird by the gobble. I have been fooled by jakes that sounded like mature birds, and I have heard mature birds that sounded like a jake. It seems to me that mature Rio gobblers sound like jakes more often than any other sub-species I hunt. I am not sure why this is the case for Rios, but it may be that the open country, where I most often hunt Rios, makes their gobble carry differently (sound muffled). At any rate, they can fool you.

Gobbler yelp—it is like the yelp of a hen but quite coarse, slower, and drawn out. I have heard mature gobblers yelp more often in the winter than in spring, and most often when they are on the roost in the mornings. It seems to be a way to keep in touch with other turkeys. Eastern Gobblers often hang out in bachelor groups during the winter and they will yelp to each other. Out west where Rios and Merriams flock up in winter, forming huge flocks, gobblers seem inclined to yelp, and like Eastern gobblers, more so in the mornings. Jake yelping is not uncommon in the spring—when they are in groups (it is common for jakes to band together). It is not unusual to hear some jakes trying to gobble, others yelping, or some doing both.

SCRATCHING NOISE

Turkeys don't make this sound with their mouths, but rather with their feet. Turkeys earn their living by scratching. They scratch up insects, seeds, masts and other food buried under leaves, straw, etc. Scratching is an audible sound that turkeys make with their legs, and it is a sound I sometimes mimic when turkey hunting. It is especially useful when birds are call shy, or you have a gobbler in close and want to convince him you are a real hen. I can do it with my hand or my foot, and not move a whole lot in doing so. Turkeys don't just scratch randomly. They scratch in a pattern. To imitate the sound of a turkey scratching, you want to simulate that pattern. I have observed my own turkeys, wild turkeys, and chickens as well, when scratching. The pattern that you want to reproduce is this: left—right—right, then pause, then left—right—right and then pause. Do it two, three, or four times, and change it up each time you do it. Turkeys scratch, look to see what turned up, often pecking up what they uncovered (the pause), then they scratch some more. Your goal is to sound like a turkey scratching, so don't just scratch—scratch—scratch—scratch—scratch. Scratch in a pattern like a turkey scratches. If you will pay attention when you are watching turkeys feed, and you surely will do so if you turkey hunt enough, you will observe how they actually scratch and feed. I like to scratch in conjunction with some contented purrs and soft clucks. At times I do nothing but scratch to entice a smart old gobbler to come the last few yards into shooting range.

CHAPTER 11
THE CLASSIC MORNING HUNT AND CALLING A GOBBLER OFF THE ROOST

The classic turkey hunt is calling a bird off the roost in the morning. This is the very basic, "hoped for" turkey hunt in spring turkey season. Say you did your scouting and found a gobbler, you made it to your spot before daylight, and you are ready to start the hunt. What do you do now? First of all, if you know from roosting him the night before exactly where he is located, you want to move into position and set up close to the bird. Close enough to hunt him, but not close enough to spook him. How fast you move to the gobbler is dictated by the situation. If at all possible, you want to be in position and set up before your gobbler leaves the roost. If a bird is gobbling on his own, simply start moving in his direction with caution. If he will gobble on his own while you move in and set up, that is the best case scenario.

If you don't know the exact location of your bird, and he is not gobbling on his own after a few minutes of listening, you should try to get him to gobble so you can get a fix on his location. Use a locator call to entice him to gobble. In the south we typically hoot like an owl to get a gobbler to sound off. In the Midwest, a coyote howler can be used to elicit a gobble from Rio and Merriam gobblers. My home in Arkansas is quite close to where gobblers sometimes roost on my creek. They will often gobble when I open and close my car door, or the garage door. It is not unusual for turkeys to gobble at a distant rooster crowing, car/truck door closing, dog barking, Canadian geese flying off their roost, gate squeaking, train whistle blowing, etc. In short, getting a gobbler to gobble on the roost in the morning is not something that takes great calling skill. It takes a loud noise! The purpose of the locator calls is to provoke a gobble so you can zero in on a gobbler's location. I don't recommend using the locator call after a gobbler starts gobbling on his own. The coyote call you should use sparingly. Remember that a coyote is a predator, so howling as you approach a gobbler's position is likely to spook him.

I like to be as close as I can get without running the risk of spooking the gobbler. Just exactly how close you get depends on the terrain, foliage on the trees, and light conditions. In open country that might be 200 yards. Note that in open country, it is important to get close before it is light enough for the turkeys to see you approaching. Their vision is great in good light, but not real good in dim light, so darkness hides your approach. If you have an open area to cross in order to get close, do it in the dark. If you must use a flashlight, use one with red lenses as red light is supposed to be undetectable to wildlife. Shine it at the ground and avoid shining it way out in front of you or in the trees. In wooded areas like pines and hardwoods, you may be able to get as close as 75 yards when trees are in full foliage and you have ground cover. As in open country, close enough may be 200 yards in open woods, like hardwoods in early spring or the Ponderosa pines in the Black Hills of South Dakota. You don't want to risk bumping the bird off the roost. If you get so close that the gobbler sees you, you probably have blown your chances of killing him. When moving in the direction of a gobbling bird, do so cautiously. Don't get in too big a hurry. You could walk right past other gobblers; all the gobblers in the area don't necessarily fire off at the same time. If your target bird is gobbling frequently, it makes it a little easier to approach him because you know his location. When close, you must find a place to set up.

Another concern during your approach is hens. You must be careful you don't run into the gobbler's hens and spook them. Quite often, especially in stage II and stage III of the breeding season, the gobblers will roost close to hens, if not right with them. I cannot tell you how many times I have ended up right in the middle of a flock of hens as I was moving in on a gobbler. If that happens, and the hens just start clucking a little, you might want to just ease back out and go around them. The gobbler probably knows where they are already. Sometimes I just sit right down amongst the hens, if I am worried I will spook them by continuing towards the gobbler or backing out. If they settle back down, things might be alright. If you back out and set up with the hens between you and the gobbler, good luck! They will probably fly out and go to him, and you will never see him. If you can get on past the hens and move a little closer to the gobbler—depends on how far he is from where you encountered the hens—do that to get between him and the hens. If you can get between the gobbler and his hens you have a better chance of killing him. If it is still pretty dark, you can probably move closer to the gobbler without spooking the hens or the gobbler. If it is getting daylight, you might spook the hens and make them fly, and the gobbler will most likely hear them fly. If they fly in the direction of the gobbler, game over! If they fly off in another direction, it can be a good thing. If the hens fly away from the gobbler, you should wait a few minutes to let things settle down. If he gobbles again, set up right there. Since he likely knew where they were, he may well come to that location right off the roost. If he does not gobble again, all bets are off. He might be looking at you, or he might have sailed off with the hens. You best just stay where you are for a bit and watch and listen for him before making your next move.

If the hens are on one side of me and the gobbler the other—I'm in the middle—I might not call at all until the gobbler is on the ground. If he hits the ground and comes my way without me calling, I might not call at all! If I do call to a gobbler on the roost, the call I usually make first is a tree yelp. It is a very short and soft yelp series. It is so soft that you can hardly hear it. If you ever get in close to a bunch of hens on the roost, you will hear them do it, so you will know exactly what it sounds like. I do the tree yelp followed by a soft cluck or two. If he gobbles at my calling, he knows where I am, and I will just shut up and wait to see what is going to happen. If I call anymore while he is on the roost, it is usually some soft clucks.

When I am set up on a gobbler and hear a hen, I know I have competition. Now, that could be a real hen, or it could be another hunter. If you hunt turkeys long enough, you will learn to tell the difference—good calling with consistent rhythm and pitch usually comes from another hunter, and rough sounding, erratic calling typically comes from real turkeys. A dead give-a-way in the south is to hear the other hunter hooting like an owl—most hunters don't sound like a real owl. If they are inexperienced, they may hoot over and over again just to hear the bird gobble.

If I have competition for the gobbler, be it a real hen or another hunter, it will influence how I call. If it is a real hen, and I am between her and the gobbler, I will usually just let her do the calling. If she is between me and the gobbler, I generally call at her, doing pretty much what she does. Remember, if she is between you and the gobbler and you cannot move around to get closer to him, that is not good, but if you can get her to come check you out when she comes off the roost, he might just come right along behind her. If I think I am competing with another hunter rather than a hen, I will generally see how the gobbler is responding to my calling and the other hunter's calling. I might just get up and leave, if I feel like I may be in harm's way. Pressured turkeys on public ground often shy away from aggressive calling, and in that case, I would probably call very little—a few soft yelps and a couple of clucks. If I am on private land, I just let the turkey dictate how much I call. I sometimes do a fly down cackle, which is like a series of really fast clucks, often starting with a yelp or ending with a yelp. I will Cackle and pat my hands against my legs rapidly to sound like wings beating as a hen flies to the ground. If you are not good at it, don't do it. You will probably just scare the gobbler off. At one time I would carry turkey wing tips (last segment containing primary feathers) and use them to make the fly down sound of wings beating. I don't do that anymore because I think I can do just about as well just patting my pant legs.

I am like most hunters in that I love to hear a turkey gobble. It is exciting, but all too often it encourages over-calling. All I want to do is let a gobbler know where I am while he is on the roost, and that does not take much calling. If you call too much, he might just sit there on the roost and wait to get a visual on a hen before he flies down. Experienced old gobblers sometimes wait until they see a hen before they fly off the roost. I had one do this time and time again behind my home. I could see him each time and easily observe what he was doing. I finally killed him, but only when I got so close to him in a thunder storm, that when he flew out to the hens he saw on the ground, I shot him in mid air. That is not the way I like to do it, but I wanted to kill that bird. Long story short, don't over call to a roosted turkey.

When a gobbler comes off the roost, there is typically a pause in the gobbling. If he has hens with him, it can be a long pause as he gets on with his business of breeding his hens. If he has no hens with him, he will usually pause for a short time then start gobbling again. The gobbling usually sounds quite different once he is on the ground—generally more muffled. The changing sound of the gobble lets you know he has hit the ground. If he is gobbling and moving in your direction, play it by ear. What you do depends on how close he is to you. If he is really close, you would probably be better off just to get your gun up, point it in the direction he seems to be coming from, and wait on him to arrive. If he responded to your call when he was on the roost, he knows your location. If he is not real close, you should probably call again. Soft yelps and clucks are advised. If he responds immediately, or cuts you off (starts to gobble while you are still making the call), you know he is interested. Wait! Resist the temptation to call every time he gobbles. If he responds to your calling, he knows where you are. Have your gun up on your knee, pointed at his line of approach, and wait for the moment of truth. If he comes on in, kill him!

When a bird is obviously on his way to you and shuts up, one of four things has probably happened. First, he may have gotten spooked somehow, by a deer, another hunter, by you, or whatever. Second, he got with a hen or hens, and something he can see with feathers trumps sweet sounds coming from "over yonder" almost every time! Third, he is on his way to you. Fourth, he just lost interest. Sometimes you never know why he stopped gobbling, he just did! If your gobbler was definitely on his way (coming in your direction) when he shut up, resist the temptation to get up and move too quickly. A gobbler will often shut up when he decides to come on in to investigate the source of the calling, looking and listening as he approaches. If he is coming to you, and you decide to get up and move, you may very well spook him. It happened to me many times, especially when I was younger and had less patience. Now, I seldom give up a position quickly. Maybe I am just lazy now, I don't know for sure. But I do stay put much longer after a bird stops gobbling. I have killed many gobblers as they came in without a peep 5 minutes or even as long as an hour after they shut up. Always keep that gun up and pointed in the direction you last heard a gobble, or where you think he might come into view. Moving too quickly is a common mistake. If you decide to call during the gobbler's "quiet time," keep it soft and keep the movement to a minimum. Always keep your eyes moving back and forth scanning the terrain for the gobbler. Over calling is another common mistake hunters make. Remember that the natural order of things is for the hen to go to the gobbler. You want to play a little "hard to get." If you call too much, he may just stop and wait for the hen to come to him. Since you are not a real hen, you cannot do that!

If the gobbler is gobbling and not coming in, he probably has hens with him, or you may just not be somewhere he cares to go. I usually stay put until I am sure that I am not in the right place to kill the bird. Never move too quickly when the bird stops gobbling. As I noted, he may be on his way. I cannot tell you how many times I scared birds when I decided too quickly to get up and move to another location, only to hear the dreaded "Putt…putt…putt," and see the back end of a gobbler making a fast exit. Shots at birds leaving like this most often end up as misses, or worse yet, in the crippling of a bird. It is best to pass on an iffy shot and hope for another chance at the bird later.

If you can tell from his gobbling, which way a disinterested gobbler is headed, you can often make a loop to get around in front of him. This is where scouting and knowing the land is important. You want to know the land well enough to know where he is, where he is going, and the route you can travel to get there before him. I hunt with guys who know their hunting grounds like the back of their hand—same way I know my hunting grounds. That knowledge is invaluable when deciding how to get around on a bird. You want to move quietly, quickly, and undetected. That may mean dropping off in a creek bed and walking in the water, slipping around a hillside to move from one hollow to the next, climbing over a mountain to reach a valley on the other side, walking across a beaver pond dam, or whatever! I tend to err on the side of caution, and if anything, make a bigger loop than necessary. If I can get around on a bird and get in front of him, henned up or not, I feel I have a good chance of killing him. When you move on a bird and arrive at the targeted location, pick a spot to set up, maybe put out a decoy or two, set up, wait a few minutes for things to settle down, then start calling again. Call very softly at first because he may be close. If he responds to your call, you are back in the ball game. Settle back into your calling routine and wait. I once moved 5 times and crossed three beaver ponds in South Georgia, before finally getting to a position that the smart old gobbler would approach. I started working that bird at daylight and killed him at 10:30 am. It took over 4 hours, and moving 5 times, but my persistence paid off.

Since I mentioned that old gobbler in Georgia, let me mention the tactic of waiting the bird out. My buddy Emory was hunting about a half mile from me that same spring morning in Georgia. He got on a smart old gobbler at daylight, and killed his gobbler about 10 minutes before I killed mine—I heard his shot. He sat in the same spot all that time and waited on that old gobbler to come to him, which he finally did. Long story short, sometimes moving on a bird works, and sometimes waiting him out is best. Emory knew the terrain and knew there were no major obstacles to prevent the bird from coming to his location. He also knew from the sounds that his bird was simply henned up. He waited him out and killed him. Waiting them out can work!

How much do you call when working a bird? That depends on the bird. I really prefer to call sparingly and wait on him to come to the gun. I like to let him gobble several times before I call again. If that is not working, I will get more aggressive, using louder yelps and some cutting. If I feel the bird is drifting off away from me, I will ratchet it up a bit with some very excited calling, perhaps even throwing in a mating cackle. I tend to adjust what I do to what the gobbler is doing. If an old hen starts talking back to me, I do my best to mimic her. If the gobbler is with her, and you can entice her to come on over to investigate the strange hen in her area, she will quite likely have the gobbler in tow. Aggressive cutting and yelping will sometimes work in this situation to fire up a boss hen. Recognize that sometimes this will backfire on you—she decides to keep him for herself and simply leads him away. There is no sure thing with turkey calling!

If a gobbler is coming to soft yelps and clucks, I keep it up and usually settle back into just clucks as he gets very close. I may do some soft purrs and scratching in the leaves if I think he is really close. If I have been calling aggressively and loud to get a gobbler to move toward me, I tend to start toning it down as he gets closer. As long as he is still coming my way, soft calling is what I do. If he cools off and seems to lose interest, I will crank it back up some to see if I can fire him up again. My buddy Lance and I once got on a gobbler up in NW Arkansas that was a bit unusual in his behavior, and thus, so were our tactics. I got him to gobble way off on some neighboring property with some loud cutting and yelping. He would respond to the loud aggressive calling, but was not coming in our direction. We moved down the field parallel to his line of movement in the woods. We set up on him several times. Each time, he would gobble a time or two at aggressive calling, but would then shut up. He just would not come to us, but instead kept on his line of movement parallel to our own movement. The woods ended at another field and we beat him around there and got set up. He gobbled at my aggressive calling, but when I toned it down he stopped gobbling and stopped coming our way. When I cranked it back up, he started coming in our direction again. I called very aggressively (I call it screaming), until I could see that bird in front of me behind a small cedar tree at 30 yards. When I toned down the calling as I normally do, he started to walk away. I started screaming at him again, and he came back. Each time I called, he would gobble and go into a strut, then come out of the strut and raise his head up to look, but he stayed behind the cedar. I kept on screaming at him until he finally stepped out in the open, and I put him down at 25 yards. Lance thought I had lost my mind screaming at that bird when he was so close, but it was what he liked. He was a 2 year old gobbler. I know for a fact that aggressive loud calling like that would have scared off a gobbler on the hard-hunted public land that I hunt in Mississippi. The moral of the story is this: you do what works for the gobbler you are hunting!

As I noted, when you hear hens with the gobbler expect your task to be harder. Calling a gobbler away from a hen is tough, but not impossible. I once called in a really nice Ozark gobbler that came running with a hen close behind doing everything she could to stop him. He was greedy, I guess! That is the exception rather than the rule. When you know your gobbler is with hens, try calling the hens to get them to bring the gobbler into gun range with them. I have killed enough gobblers this way to know it works!

At times I will hunt a roosted bird and fail to kill him—happens more often than I like. He may have gone to his hens rather than coming to my calls, just not been interested in coming to my calling location, got spooked, or whatever. I try to pay close attention to what the bird does after leaving the roost. Which way did he go? How fast was he moving? How often did he gobble? Did he hang around a while in some places along his travel route? All this information might help me later. I may have lost the battle, but maybe not the war. Often I learn enough from an encounter with a gobbler, or maybe from multiple encounters with him, to finally figure him out well enough to kill him. The truth be told, this is probably the rule rather than the exception. Very often it takes me more than one try to kill a gobbler, particularly if he is a mature gobbler and/or I am hunting unfamiliar territory.

CHAPTER 12
HUNTING GOBBLERS THROUGHOUT THE DAY

There have been many mornings when, for whatever reason, I didn't hear a gobbler on the roost, I was late getting to the woods, or I got on a gobbler and ended up empty handed. The hunt is not over just because you fail to get a bird right off the roost. There are various tactics that I use for morning hunting in the hours after fly down, and in the afternoon.

SETUP AND COLD CALL

If I am confident that there are birds in an area, and I know from the sign (tracks, scratching, dusting areas, etc.) where they like to feed and hang out, I will move to such an area, set up and start cold calling. This is a pretty good tactic in breeding phases II or III when gobblers are henned up right off the roost. I like to set up where I can see what seems to be the best line of approach for a gobbler and where I will be well hidden. I may take the time to cut a few saplings and limbs and fashion a makeshift blind for a little cover, if not much natural cover is available. If hunting the open country of Kansas or Nebraska, I usually set up around a field where birds are using. I often use decoys when using this tactic. The decoys help attract the attention of the turkeys, and they help complete the illusion—visual stimulation to go with the turkey sounds you make. I generally use a hen or two, but will occasionally use a Jake decoy as well around fields. I will say more about how to set up decoys later. After I am set up comfortably—if you are not comfortable you won't sit still, so take the few extra minutes to make sure your setup is comfortable—I start with some soft yelps and clucks. I do this just in case turkeys are close by. If after maybe 5 or 10 minutes I get no response to soft calling, I will crank it up a notch. If I still get no response for some 20 minutes or so, then I will try some aggressive calling. For aggressive calling I usually use two calls, a diaphragm and slate call most often, and I make some loud, aggressive turkey calls such as the cutting and yelping of two hens scolding each other, or perhaps a gobbler fight. I call aggressively for several minutes, then I listen for while to see what happens. The purpose of that loud calling is to see if I can evoke a shock gobble from a gobbler in the vicinity and/or just let turkeys know other turkeys are in the area. I figure that if I can get a gobbler to gobble, then the game is on! I use soft calling initially to see if he will come my way, but crank it up into more aggressive calling if necessary to get his interest. You really have to play it by ear. Never let your guard down because a gobbler will sometimes approach without so much as a peep. If you are not constantly vigilant, he could slip in on you, bust you, and be gone with you never even knowing he was there. If hens respond to my calling and come to my location, I try to carry on a conversation with them to keep them around. There is nothing quite like a live decoy! I stay in the location for usually anywhere from 30 minutes to an hour before moving if nothing is happening. If the hens hang around, I usually stay put as long as they are still present. Depending on how much confidence I have in the location, I may stay longer, or may move quicker. If I move, I will usually look for another good setup several hundred yards away and try again, or I may switch to another tactic like prospect calling.

PROSPECT CALLING

Prospect calling basically means moving through the woods and calling periodically. Some hunters call it the "cut and run" because you are using loud yelps and cutting to evoke a gobble, and covering some ground between calling stops. When you strike a gobbler, you move quickly to a position, setup, and try to call him to the gun. When I prospect call, I typically use a combination of yelping and cutting. I like to use my wingbone for prospect calling because I can get loud with it, its sound carries well, it hangs conveniently around my neck (takes little effort to get at it), and it sounds good. My second choice is my slate, but I will sometimes use a diaphragm call as well. A good box will do just fine, because the sounds of a box call normally carry a long way. My buddy Emory uses a Jake Scott "Cutter," and it carries for a very long distance. Sometimes, I just yelp, but most often I will start with some hard cutting and tail off into some aggressive yelping.

The goal of prospect calling is to raise a gobble. If the bird is very close when he responds, I try to set up quickly. I have seen birds come in so fast that I did not really have time to set up properly, so I just plopped down wherever I could—what we turkey hunters call a bad setup (excuse for failure). All too often the result of a bad setup is as follows: bird comes in, takes a look, you are pinned down and cannot shoot, and you sit helplessly as you watch him walk away. Many hunters have tried a "quick draw" shot in such circumstances only to miss or cripple a bird. If you did not spook him, you can sometimes let him walk off, then get positioned better and call him back in again—that is better than taking a bad shot and maybe boogering or spooking him. Trying to call him back once he departs is worth a try, but don't count too much on it working. To avoid this frustrating outcome, it is really a good idea to think ahead and pick a good setup spot before you ever make a call. Then you can set up quickly and set up well if a bird responds from close range. If you have to move to a distant bird, I think it is best to get him to gobble a few times to see if he is staying put in his location. If he is staying put, then you can try to cut the distance, get set up and give him a try. Once you are working the bird, how much and how often you call depends on his response. I try to call as little as possible, while still enticing him to come my way. Too much calling can cause him to hang-up and wait for you to come to him.

PROSPECTING WITH LOCATOR CALL

Prospecting with a locator involves moving through the woods trying to locate a gobbler to hunt by using a locator call. I have had success with a crow call just about everywhere I hunt because crows are nearly everywhere. Most gobblers will shock gobble at a crow flying over. A shock gobble is like a reflex for a gobbler in mating season, and many sounds will provoke a shock gobble. In the south, a Pileated woodpecker call works well as does a hawk whistle. A peacock call works well in most areas of the country—not sure why, but it does. I guess it is because it is loud, high pitched, and annoying. Coyote calls work well in the Midwest from Texas to the Dakotas. I use a coyote call out west to get them to gobble on the roost, throughout the morning, in the afternoon, in the evening after fly up; it works pretty much any time of day. Nothing is foolproof, but I always have my coyote call when hunting in the west. I hoot and crow call with my mouth, so I don't need calls for them. In the south, you sometimes hear owls on up in the day; however, if you hear an owl during the day making the exact sound over and over in most places where I hunt, it probably means you got a rookie turkey hunter nearby. Most experienced turkey hunters know better than to walk around hooting all day long! With locator calls, you are just trying to locate a gobbler. The advantage of using a locator call, rather than prospecting with a turkey call, is that you don't run the risk of calling in a bird before you are ready. Gobblers don't come to locator calls; they just gobble at them. Once you locate a gobbler, you then decide whether to set up where you are, or to cut the distance between you and him, then set up and start calling. Understand that on hard hunted public land, gobblers can learn from experience to associate some of these calls with hunters. In those cases, a locator call can cause a bird to turn tail and run the other way. Lance, Devin, and I were calling to an old gobbler one day in NW Arkansas, and he was working his way down the field toward our position—we could see him. A local yahoo stopped his pickup by the gravel road up above us, got out, and started blowing the crow call. The gobbler shut up and headed the other way. Hunt over!

THE LONG SETUP.

During stages III and IV of breeding season, I probably kill as many or more gobblers in the afternoon as I do in the morning. Gobblers that are henned up in the mornings often find themselves alone or in the company of other gobblers later in the day. Sometimes mature gobblers will sometimes have a jake or two hanging with him—their protégés. When gobblers end up by themselves during breeding season, they are vulnerable, afternoon or morning. Any of the other tactics I have discussed for hunting birds after flydown can work in the afternoon, but one of my favorite afternoon tactics is the long setup. When I know gobblers are in an area and have a chance to study them a bit, I can usually pattern them. They often have favorite places to lay up in the shade during the heat of the day, perhaps near a water hole, and they get back out to feed later in the afternoon. When I pattern gobblers and figure out their afternoon routine, I will often go where they will be hanging out and feeding in the afternoon and set up well before they get there, with the intention of staying there most of the afternoon. This works very well in the Midwest and similar areas with crops and large fields. This is really a waiting game. I will sit for hours and wait on a gobbler, if I feel confident in my location. I may call some, but not a lot. Maybe I yelp a time or two every 15 minutes or so. I typically use decoys for my long setups. If I am hunting where there are multiple gobblers, and some are mature gobblers, I may use my mature gobbler decoy that has a real turkey fan on it. It really looks like a gobbler and moves like a gobbler with the help of a little breeze. I use that gobbler with two or three hens and put them out in front of my location, typically about 20 yards from me. I like to have a comfortable chair, like my Gobbler Lounger, so I can sit comfortably and remain motionless for a long time. A good hide is necessary as well. I sometimes make a natural blind from available materials, and in some instances I use a popup blind. The key is to be able to sit still for long periods of time as you wait on your gobbler. Quite often, it is hot during the afternoons in turkey season, so I prefer to set up in the shade if at all possible. Remember that the sun is moving, so take into consideration where shade will be for the duration of your hunt. If you have done your scouting, effectively patterned your birds, have a good setup, and are patient, this tactic can be very effective even for smart old gobblers. Some turkey hunters don't think much of this tactic, but think what they may, I am here to tell you that it works.

SPOT AND STALK

Much like the spot and stalk tactic for other big game, spot and stalk for gobblers means just what it says—you spot the birds at a distance, then stalk closer to try to kill them. It can be effective morning or afternoon. When I use this tactic, I usually don't just try to sneak up on a gobbler and shoot it, although I have done it, but instead I move close enough to it to set up and call it to the gun. If I have time and can do it without being busted, I will sometimes stick out a decoy. If I can crawl through the grass and stick a decoy out without being seen, I may do it. I usually use a single Feather Flex hen that stays in my turkey vest. If I think I might get busted setting up a decoy, I don't bother with it. If I have the opportunity to watch the gobbler long enough to know what direction he is headed, it helps me pinpoint the right place to set up and kill him. If he is moving along the edge of a field, just pecking bugs or seed, he will likely continue the same course unless spooked, distracted by another turkey, or he encounters an obstacle in his way. I try to get in close and get set up. I then will call if I think it will help get the bird to come to me. If I think he will come within range without calling, I may not call at all. I have killed numerous gobblers in the Midwest using some variation of the spot and stalk. Good binoculars are a must. You don't want to spend an hour getting in position to kill a bird only to find out it is a hen or jake. Spot and stalk is a good tactic in any area where you can see for a long distance, and can use the lay of the land and available cover to hide your approach. This tactic works best if you are a skilled woodsman and know how to move undetected into position to take your gobbler.

ROOST SQUATTING

This is a late afternoon tactic. I know some of my turkey hunting buddies will ask me why I put this in my book, but it is a tactic that can work. For me, it is a tactic of last resort for killing a bird that I cannot kill another way, or to use at end of the last day I have to hunt in an area—desperate times require desperate measures! You need to know the laws in the state where you hunt to know what time you have to give up the hunt. In some states you cannot shoot past 30 minutes before sunset—know the regulations. In short, roost squatting involves waiting at or near the roost for a gobbler to return and shooting him BEFORE he flies up. I would not ever advocate shooting a gobbler on the roost. To me it is kind of like tag; when he gets in the tree, he is safe on base. I, and most turkey hunters, consider it unethical to shoot a gobbler on the roost, morning or evening, whether it legal or not. In the Midwest, more than in the areas of the south I hunt, a gobbler will return to the same spot, often the same tree, to roost day after day. If you saw where he was roosted in the morning, there is a good chance you can ambush him there in the evening. Check for gobbler droppings under likely trees to pinpoint his roost. Gobblers generally like to get to an elevated point to pitch into their roost tree. They are apt to come in to and fly from a knoll or hillside onto their roost if such terrain is available. Set up where you can see these areas, or set up in a funnel area you expect the gobbler to pass through on the way to roost. In the south, gobblers often roost on the same hillside, hilltop, hollow, or creek bottom, but not necessarily in the same tree. They love roosting around water in the south, whether it is a river, creek, beaver pond, or whatever. You can sometimes find a good place to set up on a ridge leading to a beaver pond, on top of the hill a gobbler is roosting on, or along the hillside he prefers for roosting, and wait him out. You want to be facing the direction from which you expect him to approach. Be forewarned, gobblers seem generally to be very cautious when moving toward their roost. If you are not well hidden and perfectly still, you are likely to get busted. While this tactic can help you take a bird, it does not compare the heart-thumping excitement of working a bird with a call and watching the show as an approaching gobbler struts and drums his way into gun range. That is really what spring turkey hunting is all about.

There are many other tactics that one can use to kill turkeys. I have thus far discussed pretty basic tactics. They are tried and proven tactics that many turkey hunters use—pretty conventional tactics. Later I will discuss some other tactics for killing difficult gobblers. I call them "advanced tactics" for killing gobblers.

CHAPTER 13
MAKING AN EFFECTIVE SHOT AND RETRIEVING YOUR TROPHY

Experience has taught me that there is more to making a clean kill on a gobbler than just pulling the trigger at the moment of truth. I discussed patterning your gun in an earlier chapter and that is very important. I also think that practicing with your turkey gun is important. A good pattern poorly delivered can mean a miss, or worse yet a crippled gobbler. Know your gun. That comes from patterning the gun and from practice. When you work hard and finally have that gobbler in range, you want to put him down for keeps.

At what part of a gobbler's anatomy should you aim when you get a shot at a gobbler? I will give you my opinion on it, but recognize that not everyone will agree with me. You know what they say about opinions! If everything works out perfect and you are looking down the barrel at the gobbler when he approaches, what you aim at depends on the range and your pattern at that range—that is why you should pattern your gun at different ranges BEFORE you hunt. If the bird is very, very close, say inside of 15 yards, I recommend you shoot at the base of the neck. When a gobbler walks, that old head tends to bob up and down. With the tight choke that turkey guns have today, your pattern at short range is very tight. At 10 yards, it might not be bigger than a golf or tennis ball. With a bobbing head and a tight pattern, you can easily miss at close range. I missed a gobbler at 5 yards by shooting at the head, and I did it from the same spot with the same gun, maybe on the same turkey, two years in a row. It was like reliving a bad dream. I learned from my mistakes to aim for the base of the neck on a bird so close. The base of the neck does not move around like the head, and if you hit him there at close range, he will drop like a rock.

If I am shooting at a gobbler with my old 870 turkey gun, knowing the pattern like I do, I aim at the base of his skull from 20 yards on out to about 35 or 40 yards, that way I know the spread of my pattern should put plenty of shot in the head and neck kill zones. When a bird is over 40 yards, I tend to hold on the top of his head, because my pattern will be dropping just a bit at that range. I may even move the bead just over the head if he is really on out there, say 50+ yards. I have killed birds at and around 60 yards with my 12 gauge and my 10 gauge, but don't recommend such a long shot. I won't take such a shot except under extraordinary circumstances, like when hunting wide open terrain such as an open field and a gobbler that refuses to come closer. In the wide open, I feel more confident that my whole pattern will reach him, even if it is dropping. In the woods, you often lose some of your pattern to branches, vines, and such. Still, a shot beyond 50 yards is a stretch, and you will be more effective shooting at birds well inside 50 yards. I shoot a bow, and have been judging yardage for many, many years; I use no range finder. For that reason, I am fairly confident of my ability to judge yardage, especially in the woods. Open fields often make turkeys look closer than they are, and you should take that into consideration. I have seen my hunting buddies miss more birds around fields than anywhere else, and I think that is the reason—they misjudged the yardage and shot at birds too far out! I did it myself before I learned better. Some turkey hunters I know have switched to high dollar, custom made, heavy shot shells that are supposed to produce unbelievably good patterns. My buddies have patterned their guns with such shells, and they do produce remarkable patterns. What happens though is that they have too much faith in their patterns and they shoot too darned far! My advice is to err on the safe side and don't shoot at a bird too far out. Wait and see if he will come closer. Let the gobbler leave and try to call him to another location, or hunt him another day. Whatever you do, don't run the risk of spooking him, or worse yet, crippling him by taking a bad shot.

I like to have a gobbler standing straight up, with head erect, when I take my shot. If he gets nervous when approaching, or just wants to see the hen he has heard calling to him, he will generally stop to look around, thus raising his head and offering you a good shot with the head held high and neck stretched out. If he has his head turned a little to the right or left, that is even better. That position offers full exposure of the kill zone (head and neck). To get him to stop and raise his head for you, you can cluck loudly (easy with a mouth call in your mouth), and he will generally stop and raise his head. You better be ready when you do it, because if you hesitate, he may be gone in a flash. Don't cluck until you, or your partner if hunting with someone else, is ready for the shot. A loud cluck or two will also help to bring a gobbler out of the strut for a good shot at his head.

When a gobbler is strutting, he has his head pulled down into his fluffed up feathers. That reduces your target size by hiding part of the kill zone (most of his neck). I advise against shooting a strutting gobbler, unless absolutely unavoidable, and he is close. I have seen too many birds boogered by hunters shooting at them in the strut—yes, I've done it too. Sometimes a gobbler will come in strutting and just seems not to want to come out of it. This is more likely when he has hens with him, or he is coming to your decoys. The first mature Rio I killed in Texas did that to me. He had to come under a barbed-wire fence as he approached, and he nearly tore his fan off coming under it, but he would not give up the strut. He was coming to a decoy spread comprised of a strutting jake and hen. He was fired up and ready for business, be it fighting, breeding, or both. If you must shoot a gobbler in the strut, head-on or sideways, put the bead right on the center of the head when you shoot. Again, don't take this shot unless he is close—I mean inside 25 yards even with a tight choke. A long shot at a strutting bird is a recipe for boogering a bird! I shot that Texas Rio in the strut, but he was inside 20 yards and facing me. Understand also, that when you shoot one head on, you will likely damage tail feathers, and maybe the beard; it is the price you pay!

If an incoming gobbler stops his forward progress, and starts turning his head right, then left, and/or starts to move back and forth perpendicular to your position, he's probably not coming any closer and you best take your shot. That behavior is an indication that he is nervous. Something does not seem right to him. I usually take that to mean that the gobbler is as close as he intends to come. It is show time or go time! A gobbler in this mode may start to cluck a bit, or even put. You best take your shot! As noted above, a cluck can be used to get him to raise his head for a clear shot, but if he is nervous, he might just make a hasty departure. If a bird stops and gobbles, he is not spooked. I generally prefer to wait on him to finish that gobble, then shoot. A bird sticks his head out to gobble, but when he is done he draws it back in to his body. If you are not careful, you can shoot where the head was!

I have said over and over to have your gun pointed in the direction from which you expect a gobbler to approach. If he comes in as expected, then you should not have to move your barrel much to take the shot. I generally move my barrel about as slow as a snail crawls so the gobbler does not see the movement. If possible, I move the gun when the gobbler is behind a tree in order to conceal my movement. If he stops, and I think he has made me out (spotted me) while I am moving my gun, I will swing the gun quickly to my target, stop, and shoot. If you continue to move slowly and he is spooked, you just might still be moving your barrel when he is gone. It takes good judgment to know what to do and when to do it and that comes with experience. If you move quickly to get on your bird, just be careful you don't swing past him and shoot. That can happen! Good wing-shooters learn to follow through when swinging on a flying bird, but that is not good when you are swinging on a stationary turkey.

If a gobbler approaches from an unexpected direction, as he will often do, it can be a bit of a problem. As already noted, I try to move when the gobbler steps behind a tree or something else that will conceal my movement. If you end up facing the wrong way and you have to reposition your whole body quickly, good luck! It better be a wide tree. At times it is best to just wait and hope the gobbler comes on around to a position where you can get a shot. If he is very close and does not come into your shooting window, I suggest you be patient. Don't call, just wait for the shot. You may not get a shot. It he walks away, wait until he is out of view, then move around facing the direction he went and try to call him back. Start with soft calls. It can work, but don't count on it working often. If you think you can swing quick and get the drop on a rapidly departing gobbler, guess again! I won't say you cannot make a kill this way, but the odds are against you. Most folks would be surprised just how quickly a gobbler can skedaddle, and mature gobblers seem to have a knack for keeping obstacles between you and them as they make a hasty exit. Remember, it is better to err on the side of caution and wait for another chance at a gobbler than to spook or cripple him.

I shoot left handed or right, but I am right-handed. I have practiced left-handed enough to know what I must do to shoot effectively left-handed. When I shoot my shotgun or rifle right handed, I shoot with both eyes open. I can do that and be on target because I am right-eye dominant. Most people are—it is a right handed world! When shooting left-handed, I have to remember to close my right eye, or I will pull my shot badly. A simple test can tell you which eye is dominant. Point at something with your right index finger with both eyes open. Now close your left eye. Did you stay on the object at which you pointed? If you did, then you are right-eye dominant. Most people who are right-handed are right-eye dominant. Now, do the same thing pointing with your left index finger with both eyes open, then close your right eye.

Did you move off the object? If so, this is more proof you are right-eye dominant. Reverse all variables in the test to see if you are left-eye dominant. If you are right-eye dominant, you should shoot left handed by closing your right eye. If you are left-eye dominant, you should shoot right handed with your left eye closed. If you shoot with one eye closed anyway, you still better practice with your off hand because your instinct will be to close your non-dominant eye. I once missed a gobbler when shooting left handed because he was making a hasty exit, I was in a hurry, and I failed to close my right eye. If you practice you are less likely to do the same thing. Right handed people have told me, "I cannot shoot left handed." My response is always the same, "you can if you practice." I find that I can change hands, moving my gun across my body toward a bird approaching or leaving to my right (right handed people can more easily swing to the left), with far less movement than it takes to reposition my whole body. If the bird is close but not yet in view, this is what I do. If the bird is still quite a distance away, I will reposition myself to shoot comfortably right-handed.

When do you stop shooting? This may seem like a dumb question, but it is not! If you shoot a bird well in range (close) and flat miss and can get back on your target quickly, shoot again at the head/neck area if at all possible. It is hard to kill a gobbler by body shooting him at anything but very close range, so I don't recommend it. Those feathers will turn shot, particularly at a long distance, and the vitals of the turkey offer a small target. If you shoot a gobbler and hit him, and he is obviously hit hard, then he goes down and gets up slow and addled, or goes to bouncing all over, then I suggest you keep shooting until he's down, he's out of range, or you are out of shells. You don't want a crippled bird to get away if at all possible. I will body shoot a gobbler in this situation if that is all I have for a target. I have killed a truck load of gobblers, and I can count the number of gobblers I killed with a second or third shot on one hand. Long story short, if you take only good, high percentage, shots, follow up shots shouldn't be necessary.

If you shoot and the bird goes down, spreads his fan and wings out, and is not bouncing or anything, you should stand up quickly with gun ready and move quickly to the bird. I generally shuck a shell from my old 870 by reflex right after the first shot, getting ready for another if necessary. You should do whatever you must do to be ready for a second shot. I generally approach the bird with gun ready and put my foot on his neck near the base of the neck, so when he starts the death flop, which is pretty much normal, he won't damage his fan. If he is flopping after you shoot, I recommend you get up quickly and get to him as fast as you can, but be careful with that loaded gun! If you are hunting with someone else, make sure they know what you plan to do after the shot so they don't shoot you. Be ready for another shot if it is necessary. When you get to where he is flopping, move in and get your foot on his neck as described above. It is not always easy, since he may be flopping all over the place. Sometimes getting to them is not that easy. I had gobblers flop down the side of a mountain, flop into a creek, flop into a thicket, and more. Be ready at all times to shoot again! I have seen more birds run or fly off coming out of a flop, than I have from that "spread eagle" position I described. If the downed gobbler is squatted with his head up, you really better be careful. When they are in that position, I generally shoot again. If, with my foot on his neck, a gobbler is not dying quickly, I will take my other foot and step on his head, pressing down firmly. The skull of a turkey is pretty thin, so it is not hard to crush it. You don't generally have to stomp on the head and doing that can make your gobbler look pretty ugly when you take pictures.

I suggest you DO NOT reach down and grab the bird until he is stone dead. If you are too hasty and grab a gobbler, and he then goes to flopping and twisting, he can hurt you. Remember that those spurs are weapons and can be pretty danged sharp. I grabbed a mature bird by his leg when I was young and foolish, and he started twisting in my hand. I had on some cotton jersey gloves. He got a spur caught up in my glove and tore a good size gash in my palm. I could not get loose from him because the spur was hung in my glove. It hurt, and I still have the scar! Many turkey hunters have made that mistake once, but few are foolish enough to do it a second time.

A gobbler is a lot stronger than you think, and even a flogging with the wings is something to be avoided. They won't cut you, but they don't feel good! I will tell you little story about the strength in those wings. When I was in college, an elderly neighbor lady and I would get together and kill chickens for the freezer each fall. She had an old gobbler to kill one fall. We always tied chickens upside down from her granddaughter's swing set and cut their throats. They would hang there, flapping their wings, until they bled out and died. I hung up that old gobbler and cut his throat, and when he started flopping, I thought he was going to pull the swing set anchors out of the ground. That whole swing set was rocking and rolling like a rocket taking off as he flapped those powerful wings. Long story short, be careful when you pick up your gobbler. Do it when he is stone dead and not before.

If you booger a bird (cripple him), and he heads off kind of addled and unstable, and you can get to him quickly, do so and shoot him again. If that is not possible, then watch him to see where he goes and don't follow too quickly. He will likely not go far before squatting somewhere under a bush, by a log, or something; he will try to hide. I shot a gobbler in Kansas a few years ago right after flydown. He had a hen with him and would not come out of the strut, no matter what I did. I shot him at about 30 yards and he bounced around then headed straight away (note: the back of the head of a gobbler at a distance is not a good target—small kill zone), looking very addled and wobbly-legged. I was unable to get after him quickly enough to get another shot, so I watched carefully as he headed off into some tall grass across the big food plot I was hunting. He disappeared into a large grassy area shaped like a big bowl, with dead grass in it about waist high. I watched for a while, probably 15 minutes, and never saw him come up out of the bowl. The grass was not tall on top, and I could see all around it. I walked to where I shot him and saw lots of feathers, so I knew he was hit pretty good. I left him and hunted for an hour or so, then returned to look for him. I then walked into the grassy area where I saw him disappear. He had started in on a deer trail, so I walked down that trail very slowly looking the area over very well as I walked. About 30 yards in, I spotted him squatted down in the grass with his head up facing away from me. His head was bloody and he was obviously hurt bad. I took no chances and shot him again. I recovered that nice Kansas trophy.

If a bird escapes dragging a wing, or leg, but is moving fast as if that injury is all that is wrong with him, I will give chase immediately. If he cannot fly, he can still run fast and you probably won't run him down, but you may get another shot as he goes down and up a hill, or gets slowed down by heavy brush or some other obstacle. If his leg is crippled and his wings are not, he will probably fly off. I will get to that! I know you are thinking that running with a loaded gun is dangerous, and you are right. I guess I should say don't do it, so I will say it—don't do it! With that said, I will continue telling you what I do. If a gobbler gets away from me like this, I will mark the last place I saw him and then start to look for him very carefully, with gun ready in case he jumps up in front of me. My buddy Emory and I retrieved a bird in this way many years ago. It was Emory's second gobbler, we were young, and we wanted that gobbler bad. After Emory shot him, the gobbler jumped up and took off across a little bottom, then over the next hill. We immediately gave chase. He ran into a swampy area by a beaver pond. I followed his tracks into the bulrushes while Emory waited on the hardwood hill overlooking the swamp. Emory could see me clearly, so there was no danger of him shooting me. When I walked up on the wounded bird, he jumped up in front of me and ran back up past Emory. Emory shot at him again and missed him. With a now empty gun, Emory watched as the bird escaped into a pine thicket at the top of the hill. We swapped guns, so that Emory now had a loaded gun, and started the search again making circles like we would do to pick up a blood trail for a wounded deer. We hollered at each other to keep in touch for safety sake. I found that gobbler hunkered down under some rabbit cane and honey-suckle. I was now holding the empty gun and Emory was several hundred yards away with the loaded gun. I hollered at Emory and he came back to my location to deliver a fatal shot to that gobbler. We got him! In this case, giving chase quickly and persistence paid off.

I want to relay another wounded bird story. Long years ago I shot a mature gobbler on the edge of a field with a single shot 12 gauge and 7 ½ shot. I did not plan on hunting that day, so I had only one shell. I was scouting and had carried the gun for snakes; we had rattlesnakes on the farm where I hunted. Well, the bird came out with a flock of hens not 25 yards from me. They then saw me, turned, and headed back the way they came. The gobbler was last in line and was not moving too very fast. I had a good close shot, and season was in, so I took it. The gobbler took off into the woods, but was obviously hard hit. I never lost sight of him. I got in after that bird like a duck on a June bug and hemmed him up in some bramble briars after a short sprint—I could run faster back then. I had to beat him to death with the barrel of my gun, but I got him. The situation required a quick decision and fast action, and I got my bird.

If you hit a bird and he flies off, watch to see what direction he flies. You may see him or hear him go down. If you do, go to that spot and start looking as I have suggested. Look very slow and carefully, and you may just find him. I know people who have found crippled birds in this manner, so it can work. I would offer this word of caution. When you find him, don't hesitate to shoot him again. My buddy Ed did this one time in Texas. He walked up on his bird that had crash landed in a dirt road. Ed was standing there admiring the bird's beard rather than shooting him again, and he did not have his gun ready—it was now empty. As he watched, that turkey jumped into the air like he was fired from a cannon, and took off flying, never to be seen again. So, when you find a wounded bird, shoot first and admire the beard later!

My point about cripples is as follows: what you do with a crippled bird depends on the situation and requires some fast thinking, and sometimes swift action. Other times the situation requires restraint and patience. If you lose a bird and simply cannot find him by searching the area, you might try a dog. A good bird dog or retriever can sometimes find a crippled turkey—they are just big birds. So, if you lose a bird and have access to such a dog, give it a try. It may save your trophy. I once had an old Irish Setter named Cyclone that could find anything, even a rock under water, so putting him on a lost gobbler was a no brainer. Cyclone found wood ducks for me that had been hiding under marsh grass for hours after I shot them. You don't want to lose a bird if there is anything you can do to prevent it. I will close the discussion of cripples by saying that I have found few birds that I crippled. That is the truth! I always look, but I am seldom successful. That is why it is so important that you <u>take only a good shot and make the shot good</u>!

CHAPTER 14
USING DECOYS AND BLINDS

Turkey decoys are legal is most states, but not all. Some states allow them, but have management areas where they are not allowed. It is important that you know the regulations where you intend to hunt and obey the law.

DECOYS

I discussed various types of decoys in the chapter on equipment. I also mentioned using decoys in discussing turkey hunting tactics. Here I will try to shed some additional light on how you might use decoys effectively. There is more to using a decoy, or decoys, than just pushing a stake down in the ground and hanging the decoy on it. Any good duck hunter will tell you that there is a right way and many wrong ways to set out a decoy spread. I believe it is the same with turkey decoys. Also like ducks, when turkeys have encountered decoys and been fired upon, decoys can signal danger causing turkeys to shy away from them. Perhaps turkeys are not quite as picky as ducks, but old gobblers aren't stupid and they have excellent vision.

First let me say, I generally prefer not to use decoys when I am calling a gobbler off the roost in most places I hunt. Decoys are just something else to carry, and require more time and movement when setting up. If the terrain is right, and I set up properly, a decoy is not usually needed. Light at fly-down time in the early morning is dim, so I don't think gobblers see decoys particularly well at a distance. That said, I generally have a light weight, fold-up hen in my vest just in case I need it later in the day.

If I have little choice but to set up in a big open hollow, or along the edge of a field where the gobbler will be able to see where the calling is coming from before he is in range, the visual stimulation of a decoy may be the trick that brings a gobbler to the gun. A decoy, or decoys, can attract a gobbler's attention and take it off of you. If I use a single decoy, it will be a hen, and I will set it out in front of me, usually at about 20 yards. I try to get the stake in the ground straight, and about the right depth, so the decoy does not lean in an unnatural way or look like it is on stilts or sitting on the ground. I want it to look real! If the wind is blowing hard, I sometimes use a stake next to the decoy's tail to keep it from blowing around in circles in an unnatural fashion. You can push a stake in the ground, at the tail end of the decoy opposite the side from which the wind is blowing, and limit its movement. I have used two stakes for this purpose, putting one on one side of the tail and another on the opposite side, simply to limit the decoys range of motion. A decoy spinning in circles on the stake is not lifelike! If I expect the bird to come from my left, I don't put the bird right in front of me, but more to my right, so the bird looks past me to where the decoy is located. Again, I want the gobbler's attention on the decoy and not me. What looks real? Observe live hens and you will see what looks realistic. How do they stand, how do they feed? Where do they stand and where do they feed? The more you observe and understand turkey behavior, the better you should understand how to set up a decoy, or several of them, in a manner that is lifelike.

Always consider the possibility of another hunter approaching and shooting at your decoy. Think about where the pattern would travel if that happened? I try to position my decoy such that, if another hunter does approach and shoots at my decoy, the shot would not come in my direction. In short, I want to see a long way past my decoy when looking in the direction of my decoy—ideally further than a shotgun blast would carry. This is particularly important when hunting on public ground. Safety should always be a primary concern.

Using multiple decoys can have its advantages. I use multiple decoys primarily when I am hunting open areas and have plenty of time to set up. I may use a couple of hens, and sometimes use two hens and a gobbler and/or jake. If I am certain the gobbler in the area is a dominant gobbler, I often use my life-like mature gobbler decoy. It has taxidermy eyes and a realistic head, and it looks very real with the feather fan on it and a little breeze to give it movement. It looks and moves very much like a live gobbler. If I think there may be 2 year olds in the area, and want to take one of them or a mature gobbler, I tend to use a jake decoy in my spread. A mature gobbler decoy can intimidate 2 year olds and scare them off. If in doubt, I use the jake! A jake decoy won't likely intimidate even another jake. My jake decoy is a B-mobile Jake by Primos, and it has a silk jake fan. The jake decoy is not much bigger than a hen, and it, like my mature gobbler decoy, moves around some on the stake with a breeze thus making it lifelike. A jake with a couple of hens can be a very effective setup for just about any gobbler. Recognize that it takes a while to set them up, and you have quite a bit of baggage when you carry 3 decoys in with you. I use this setup much more often in the Midwest than I do in the hardwoods of the south, but it can be effective anywhere. I have seen gobblers run across a field to my gobbler with hens decoy spread.

I pay attention to detail when I set up a single decoy or a spread. With a single hen, I try to position her in the right direction from me and set her up to look realistic. With my 3 decoy spread, I typically use a hen in the breeding position and put it right in front of the jake or gobbler decoy, maybe a few feet away. My jake/gobbler is generally facing the breeding hen's rear as she is facing away from him, so it looks like he is approaching to breed her. I will have another hen set out to the side maybe 12 to 15 feet in a feeding position. Sometimes I use just the jake and a single feeding hen. I have used the jake and the mature gobbler with two hens and put the jake out to the side, like he is watching the mature bird do his thing. The key is to make the spread look natural. Don't put your decoys in a tight little wad, because that does not look natural. Learn what looks natural by observing real turkeys when you get the chance. There is no better way to learn about turkey behavior than to watch and listen to real wild turkeys.

This is a jake with feeding hen spread used in Oklahoma. The terrain is wide open and gobblers can see the spread from a long way off. I set up against the tree in the upper right hand corner of the picture about 20 yards from the decoys.

I mentioned safety in your setup already, but if you use a gobbler decoy, you should be particularly careful. Gobblers are what hunters are looking to shoot! I seldom use gobbler decoys on public land because it is so dangerous. I use them much more often on private land when I pretty well know who is hunting around me. I still set them up in a direction that minimizes the chances of me getting shot by a hunter who I might not see approach.

The decoy spread I described above works well in conjunction with a blind in open country and can be helpful in getting birds into bow range. Because when bow hunting you have to move to draw the bow, the decoys can be helpful in drawing attention away from your position, and the blind conceals your movement. The more a gobbler's attention is focused on the decoys, the less likely he is to see you. Decoys and blinds help to put the odds in the bow-hunter's favor and make possible better shot opportunities.

I've had gobblers run right in, ready to jump on my gobbler decoy, and I killed them before they had the chance to! The first time I used my mature gobbler decoy in Kansas, I missed a big gobbler because he ran in so fast I was not ready for him. I've seen several mature gobblers come running in, knock over my jake, and just go nuts gobbling and fighting among themselves. I've had two and three hens come into my decoy spread and spend the whole afternoon among them, acting like they enjoyed the company of my decoys—there's nothing like live bait! In short, decoys can be very effective, but you need to be attentive to how and when you use them. Make your decoys look real to put the odds in your favor, and always put safety first!

BLINDS

Blinds can be an effective tool for turkey hunting. I use blinds on occasion and they work well. I have two blinds. One of them is a "one man" blind, and with a comfortable chair, I can sit comfortably in that blind for a long period of time. I use it most often in open country where hiding places are scarce, and I use it when it is raining. It is a pop up blind, so it takes only a couple of minutes to set up and take down. That is handy! While it is not water proof, it is water resistant and keeps me drier than I would be if I were sitting out in the rain. My other blind is a large blind that will handle two or three people. It is 60 X 60 X 84, giving me plenty of room to stand up. I use it when I know someone else will be hunting in it with me. This one is part pop-up, in that the 4 walls pop up, but you then have to insert poles to push the roof up. It takes probably 10 to 15 minutes to set up and just a bit less to take down. Both of these blinds have carrying cases with straps so they can be carried like a back pack. I don't like to carry either one of them very far without help, because I have to carry a chair or chairs, and often decoys as well.

Both of my blinds are black on the inside which is important because it makes it more difficult for a bird, or deer for that matter, to see you inside the blind. If you are buying a blind, this is something to look for—black out! You should also wear something that blends into the darkness of the blind—dark camo or black works best. A light colored camo pattern is not ideal because you may stick out like a sore thumb. I generally wear a fairly dark camo pattern as opposed to black because I may very well decide to move to a position outside the blind. I know people who wear black inside their blinds, but they don't anticipate hunting anywhere but their blinds. My point is that what you wear inside the blind does matter!

How and where you set up a blind depends on the terrain, the turkeys, and the hunting pressure. If you are hunting an area where hunters routinely use pop-up blinds and turkeys know one when they see it, you should conceal it well. You can set up your blind and brush it in well—hang brush and such on it and stand brush up around it to conceal it—so that it does not look like a blind; you can back it into some fairly dense cover like a plum thicket; or you can set it up in a heavily shaded area so it won't be obvious. I have found that setting my blind up under a tree with lots of low-hanging limbs works well for me. The tree does not have to be a big tree, but should have limbs coming down to the top of the blind to break up its outline. I use a pruner and/or knife to cut little trees or bushes, limbs, corn stalks, etc., to brush in my blind. To hide a blind you want to break up the outline of the blind so it blends into the available cover and does not look like a blind. In windy areas, you may have secure the stuff you use to brush it in by tying it to the blind, weaving it together, or sticking it in the ground so it won't blow away. I carry string in my blind bags for that purpose, and some blinds have ties on them. You might be surprised at what a 30 mph wind will do to your good hide. Also, you should probably stake the blind down well, or the whole thing might go flying. I have cut holes in thickets using my pruner in order to back my blind into a thicket to hide it. If turkeys are leery of blinds in the area you are hunting, you better hide it well, or they may avoid it.

On left: hub style blind backed up in trees and brushed in. On right: teepee style pop-up blind backed into a plum thicket in a Nebraska cornfield and brushed in. Neither is completely concealed, just made to blend in with the surroundings.

In some areas turkeys are oblivious to the presence of a blind. They will walk right up to a blind and feed all around it as if it were not there. In such cases, doing a lot of work to brush it in may not be necessary. In an area where there is no cover and turkeys have not learned to shy away from blinds, you can stick a blind in the middle of an open field and use it effectively. I have seen hunting videos where that is routinely done, but to be honest, I never do that myself. I try to make my blind blend in no matter where I use it. When you hunt places like I hunt, and opportunities to kill a gobbler don't come along one right after the other, you don't want anything to cost you an opportunity to kill a gobbler. I like to make sure the blind is hidden and that it hides me, so that no opportunities are missed. My advice, therefore, is that you make an effort to see that your blind blends in!

Inside your blind you will typically need chairs. I like to have chairs that are comfortable, because if I am hunting a blind, I probably plan to hunt it all morning or all afternoon. Chairs should also be fairly convenient to carry, since you often have to carry them for a distance, along with other equipment. Many come with a carrying bag you can sling over your shoulder. The chairs should be tall enough for you to easily shoot out of the blind, but no so tall that they make your silhouette easy to see from outside the blind. Basically, that means the windows or holes you will shoot through should be about shoulder high when you sit in your chair. Check it out and know before you go! When hunting in a blind, you want to position your chair in your blind to allow you to shoot out whatever windows or opening will afford you a view of approaching turkeys. Blinds have various types of windows and openings to shoot through. Ideally, the windows are open such that a turkey will not see your silhouette when approaching the blind, yet they facilitate a good shot at an approaching turkey. I like to get just the end of my barrel out of the blind when shooting from a blind, so the gunshot does not burst my ear-drums, but I don't want to have to stick the whole barrel out and run the risk of a turkey seeing it. That means positioning your chair back away from the windows. Check it out before a turkey arrives—sit in your chair, raise your gun and point it out different windows and see how it works, repositioning the chair if necessary, or opening/closing openings as necessary. When I am hunting from a blind, I do this as soon as I get inside the blind to hunt. If you intend to hunt with a bow, the same holds true for positioning yourself properly inside the blind. I recommend you practice shooting your bow from inside the blind. Practice while standing up and sitting down, so you can do either as needed. Everything has to be perfect for success when bow hunting turkeys, or even deer for that matter. You better have the right equipment, practice a lot, develop a good plan, and execute the plan perfectly. Every little detail is even more important when bow hunting turkeys.

If two people are hunting from a blind, good planning and coordination are even more important. Decide who does what, when, where and how before turkeys show up. Have everything you need before you go, like enough chairs and enough room in the blind. Decide who shoots turkeys approaching from different directions. Get everything organized when you get in the blind so everything works well for both hunters. If you hope to get a double, have a plan for it. When my buddies and I hunt together in a pop-up blind, we normally decide who shoots birds coming from the left, and from the right, and how we will handle it when there is more than one gobbler. We always have a shooting signal whether it is a countdown, or some signal involving turkey sounds. If you do it right, and both shoot at gobblers at the same time, it should be so well scripted, that it sounds like one shot rather than two shots. Emory and I have pulled this off perfectly, but we have been hunting together for 30 years. Lance and I have done it as well, always getting at least one bird, but not always two. The key to success with doubling on gobblers is good planning.

On occasion I will build a blind from which to hunt. I think one constructed from scratch is more realistic, but it is also more time consuming and does not hide you quite so well. I did it before I had a pop-up blind, and I still build a blind on occasion because the location I intend to hunt lends itself better to a natural blind. That can be because there is not a good way to conceal a pop-up, the area I intend to hunt is too far back to carry a pop-up, I intend to hunt the spot over and over, or there is just plenty of good cover to start with. Some natural blinds take only a few minutes to construct and consist only of a few bushes or saplings cut and stuck in the ground around me to conceal my position, and some take a bit more time and effort. For these I like to build them next to a tree. I will start with placing limbs or saplings up against a tree like a tee-pee and then lean more and more material against it to create the blind. I typically leave a sizable opening facing the area from which I expect a bird to approach. Sometimes I can use a blow-down or bushes. I then lay limbs or saplings horizontally across the limbs or bushes, to get somewhat of a frame against which I lean more limbs, saplings, corn stalks, etc., vertically to complete the blind. A blind, or "hide" as my Yankee friend Doug calls it, like this can provide concealment and can look very natural. A downside of these blinds is that it is quite often difficult to shoot a bird that comes from an unexpected direction because you cannot move around to shoot like you can in a pop-up.

Natural blinds work! Steven, a hunting buddy of mine, and I were in a natural blind we constructed of mesquite on a west Texas ranch, when we had a huge Rio gobbler come to us. I have never been so close to a live wild gobbler! That bird was so close that I could have reached out and touched him with my hand. Steven was on my left in the blind, and the turkey was on my right, just outside the blind, about 3 feet from us. Neither of us could get a gun up to shoot him, so we just watched him strut, drum and gobble (almost busted my ear drum because he was so close). I was watching out the corner of my eye, and Steven was looking straight at the bird. We got so tickled we almost started laughing at our situation. That old Rio stood there for what seemed like an eternity, then finally turned and walked back the way he came, with neither of us able to get a gun up to shoot. We soon after had a herd of about 20 wild hogs come up right behind us, within a few feet, and they never knew we were in the world. My point is that natural blinds can be very effective concealment. Just be sure you correctly anticipate the direction from which the bird will approach, or at least try your best!

Be careful about leaving a blind in a field with livestock. A friend of mine in South Dakota allowed some turkey hunters to hunt on his place, and they hunted from a pop-up in his horse pasture. When they came out for the day, they left the blind in place so they could hunt it the next day. Doug told them the horse might get it, but they ignored his warning. Shortly after they left, Doug watched as his young gelding grabbed up the pop-up blind, throwing it back over his head, and took off up the hill with it. When the gelding finally got it off of him, there was not much left but hoops and pieces of camo material scattered about the horse pen. The hunters acted surprised the next day when they returned and found their blind in pieces. Doug laughed! Livestock, both horses and cows, can be very curious, and they may destroy your blind be it a pop-up or a natural blind. Be forewarned, it can happen!

CHAPTER 15
ADVANCED TACTICS FOR TAKING GOBBLERS

In this section I will explain some advanced tactics for gobblers. When more traditional tactics don't work, you need some tricks in your bag. Here are some that I use. They have helped me kill some smart old gobblers!

GOING WHERE HE WAS

When a gobbler hangs up, it is usually because he has hens with him, an obstacle has impeded his progress toward you, you are not where he wants to go, or he is just smart and expects the hen to come to him. On numerous occasions I have had gobblers hang up and do the usual gobbling, strutting and drumming, then move off, only to return to the previous location again after a short while and go through the same thing again. I have hunted gobblers that would do this over and over, but would not come to my position. When a gobbler does this, a good tactic is to go where he was! Once I figure out that a gobbler is playing this game, I try to move on him when he moves off. I try to move quickly and quietly to his last location, pick a good setup, and start calling again. Depending on the terrain, I may set out a decoy, normally just a single hen decoy. I do some soft calling and wait a few minutes to see if he will respond. If he gobbles and starts toward my position, then a little soft calling and silence usually does the trick. He knows where the calling is coming from, and if he has a mind to come, he will. If he does not respond for a good while—you can gauge that from his behavior before he moved off—more aggressive calling is in order. I will cut loose with some aggressive yelps, and cutting to say to him in turkey talk, "okay big boy, I came to you; where are you now?" This tactic has worked for me on numerous occasions, but nothing works all the time. If I don't take the gobbler that day, I will usually try to be in his spot before he gets there that next day—the location where he was doing all the gobbling. I have killed many smart old gobblers by meeting them in the location of their choice, essentially by patterning them.

Woodsmanship is important in executing this tactic for several reasons. First, you must be able to pinpoint from the sound where your bird is gobbling and displaying, and know how to get there without getting busted. Knowing the area helps greatly, and in particular knowing the terrain and how to use it in your favor while making your move. Second, you must recognize when you get to the spot where the bird was gobbling. Often you will find scratching in that spot because he had hens with him, and that may very well be the reason he would not come to your calling—while he was gobbling, his hens were scratching around feeding. I have been hunting turkeys for so long that I have learned to "think like a turkey." I think I can tell just by the look of a place if it is likely to be where the gobbler was located while he was doing his gobbling, strutting and drumming. You may find drag marks (from strutting) in the dirt, sand, or leaves to confirm that you found his spot. Third, moving quickly and undetected through the woods in spring, particularly in early spring when the woods are open, requires woodsmanship. You need to know how to walk quietly and use available cover as you move stealthily through the woods like an animal. I am convinced that hard hunted turkeys know what an upright man looks like, so when I cross an opening where I think a turkey may spot me, I lean forward, hunker down, and attempt to present a silhouette that resembles a cow, deer, or hog moving through the woods. When I was a child, my dad taught me how to quietly stalk through the woods while squirrel hunting. You put your heel down first, then you ease the front of your foot down (heel—arch—toe). You can feel limbs and sticks under your feet before snapping them, and thus avoid making loud, unnatural noises. You basically feel your way along with your feet. This is how I walk quietly. I can sound more like a deer walking through the woods than a human. Many hunters will trip over stuff, break limbs, kick stuff out of the way, allow limbs and vines to noisily rake across their clothing, etc., and thus they sound like a truck going through the woods. I have hunted with people like this, and I can tell you that moving quietly with them is impossible. Moving on a bird is easier if you are alone. More hunters on the move just increase your chances of spooking the bird. If the other person with you is also a good woodsman, it is not so bad! When Lance and I do this, and we do it fairly often, as we approach what we think was the gobbler's position, only one of us moves at a time. The other stops, watches and listens as the other moves. I think this is the best way for two to move on a gobbler.

DOUBLING UP ON GOBBLERS

At times you can fool an old gobbler by doubling up on him with another good hunter—two hunters who work well together can sometimes kill a smart gobbler easier than one good hunter. Doubling up is also a good way to score a double (each hunter takes a turkey). Doubling up is also a good tactic for enjoying time in the turkey woods with a good friend and for teaching new hunters the fine art of turkey hunting. Hunting with another hunter, if done right, can make the experience of turkey hunting even more enjoyable. There are numerous ways and reasons to double up on gobblers. I will elaborate on some of them here. I know they work because I have used them.

Caller Back/Shooter Forward. This doubling tactic is effective at times on mature old gobblers that just won't come that last little distance to the gun, hanging up just out of range. They generally do this because they are waiting for the hen to come to them. I have hunted wise old birds that operated this way, and they can be hard to kill. This tactic also works for doubling on a bird you are calling off the roost. When you use the Caller back-Shooter forward tactic, one hunter (the shooter) sets up in the forward position close to the location where you expect the gobbler to approach—this is usually known from previous experience with the bird. The other hunter (the caller) sets up further back to do the calling. The distance between the hunters depends a lot on the terrain, but somewhere between 50 and 100 yards probably works best. If the hunters are too far apart, the bird might circle the forward hunter and approach the caller. That is okay if the caller has a gun and the bird is not in between the two hunters. When my buddies and I do this, we always make visual contact for safety sake—forward hunter waves a hand when in position, then the caller acknowledges the wave with a nod, wave, or thumbs up. Safety is critical in turkey hunting because both hunters are wearing camo head to toe. Failure to take this precaution could cause either hunter to be reluctant to shoot a bird that approaches for fear of hitting the other hunter, or worse yet, one could shoot the other by mistake. I don't generally use decoys with this tactic, but if used, placement of the decoy(s) should take into consideration where best to lure the bird for a good shot opportunity as well as safety. The forward hunter must remain motionless, and vigilant, if he/she is going to get a shot when the gobbler approaches. The turkey might gobble, but then again he might not. Basically, the back caller does the calling and the forward hunter does the shooting—the ideal outcome. The tactic works well when you have patterned the bird enough to know where the forward hunter should be positioned. Often this is the location of hang-ups during previous hunts. Bow hunters sometimes find this a good way to get a shot at a turkey when they are not using a blind. In that case, the caller attempts to call the turkey past the shooter (with a bow in this case), giving the archer a shot at a gobbler that is making his way to the hen sounds. This can give the archer a chance to draw the bow while the gobbler is focused on something besides his/her location. The Caller back/Shooter forward tactic belongs in your bag of tricks for tough gobblers. I will not call this technique fool proof, but I have been party to successful hunts using this tactic.

The Noisy Flock. Another doubling tactic, this is a favorite tactic of mine for late morning and afternoon hunting in stages II and III of the breeding season. I double up with Lance more than anyone else I hunt with, so much in fact that we don't even have to communicate with anything but turkey talk and maybe a hand signal or two while hunting. When I hunt with most people, we hunt together but separate; we go off in different directions. I don't feel like I reduce my chances of taking a bird when hunting with Lance, and if we are hunting in the same area, we generally hunt together even when going after a bird on the roost. Our goal is always to get the bird, and neither of us much care who does the shooting. It is just that way with us! Of course we have hunted together for 18 years now, and we have killed lots of gobblers as a team. My point is this: it helps for two hunters to be on the same page when employing the noisy flock. That comes from experience hunting together.

I feel comfortable employing the noisy flock with only a small number of my hunting buddies, simply because we have hunted together so much, it just feels right. This is how it works. We set up in an area, morning or afternoon, where we know there are turkeys, or we find them by prospecting. We usually set out a spread of decoys consisting of at least one gobbler, usually a jake, and two or three hens. We call together, softly at first just in case a bird is close. If there is no response to our soft calling, we call aggressively, and I do mean aggressively, in an effort to get a gobbler to respond! We often ratchet up the calling to some real aggressive yelping, cutting, and even some aggressive purring like two hens scolding each other. Occasionally we will throw in a gobble and even the sounds of a gobbler fight (aggressive purring and wings flapping). The idea is to convince a gobbler that there is a party going on in his area without him! Lance and I have killed quite a few gobblers with this tactic. We usually set up close together, within 20 yards of so of each other, covering different approach routes with the decoys out in front of us. The shooting plan needs to be worked out in advance. Our rule of thumb for shooting is as follows: hunter on the right takes a bird coming from the right, hunter on the left takes a bird coming from the left, and if two gobblers come up, we take the bird on our own side (left or right). If the goal is to get one of the hunters a gobbler, he gets the best position and if at all possible, the shot. Achieving a double requires effective coordination of the shot which I have mentioned before; you need a plan for synchronizing the shots. In calling, the two callers basically talk to each other in turkey talk, like two hens would do. After getting loud, what we do next depends on whether we hear a gobbler and how he responds. If a gobbler responds, gobbling two or three times at our noise, and seems hot, we will then tone it down to some turkey small talk and wait to see what he is going to do. We can usually tell if he is coming in by his gobbling, and if he is, we play it by ear. If we get no gobble with our noisy calling, then we engage in some turkey small talk for a little while, like 5 or 10 minutes, then we ratchet it up to aggressive calling again. When a gobbler does respond and starts gobbling, we can usually tell which caller's calling he prefers. We don't have to talk about it, we just know from hunting together. In this case, one caller takes charge and tries to work the bird on in, with the other caller just accompanying as needed to coax the gobbler on into shotgun range. Lance and I have used this tactic effectively on numerous occasions. Gobblers often gobble less in the afternoons, and will sometimes come in without a peep, so you must be always ready for a gobbler to approach—don't be moving around. Lance and I both know to stay still, and I honestly cannot recall either of us ever getting busted when employing this tactic. I cannot emphasize enough the importance of the two hunters working in concert. This tactic works best when hunters really know and trust each other and each other's abilities. I have done this with Emory, Tim and Ed as well. Emory and I usually get to hunt together only once every year or two, but we still can pull this off. We once had a string of successful hunts that included taking two singles and a double. The streak did not last, but it sure felt good and gave us great confidence in the tactic. My buddies and I have killed quite a few birds using the noisy flock tactic.

 One afternoon Lance and I got on a bird that we had hunted that morning, only to have him go off on the neighbor's land where we could not follow. We sat down and started with our noisy flock, and he gobbled immediately, but from several hundred yards away on the neighbor's place and across a small creek. We cranked it up and he would gobble and gobble, but would not budge from his position. He finally came down into the hollow, stopping at the creek where he gobbled, and gobbled, and gobbled. At that point we decided to give him the silent treatment—I will say more about this tactic later. We just shut up and scratched in the leaves a little. He kept gobbling on his own for a few minutes, then shut up. I clucked a time or two a few minutes later, and he gobbled about a hundred yards down the hill. We could hear him drumming as well. A minute later we saw him strutting up the hill. He never came out of the strut except to gobble as he worked up that hill to our location. We had decoys out in front of us about 15 yards away. He was angling up the hill the other side of Lance and apparently had not seen the decoys. I clucked softly to get his attention and he looked in our direction, spotted the decoys (two jakes—one strutting, one not) and two hens, and nearly broke his neck trying to get through a hole in a hog wire fence below the decoys. Lance nailed him. The noisy flock got his interest, but the silent treatment got him killed. He had to see what happened to all those turkeys, and it was his last party! From beginning to end, that hunt probably lasted at least two hours. Lance and I used slate calls, box calls, diaphragms, and finally scratching in the leaves, to make the turkey noise that fooled that smart old bird.

Buddy Blind Hunting. My buddies and I have used this doubling tactic often in morning or afternoon hunting for Rios in Texas, Oklahoma and Kansas. It can work for Easterns and Merriams as well, but I think it is be best suited to open terrain, so it is effective around fields, on open prairie, etc. I find those conditions common in my Midwest hunting grounds, and so use it most often out there. With this tactic, you find a good location for the blind through scouting to locate a high traffic area. You can do this by reading sign (tracks, droppings, strut marks and scratching). I prefer to actually watch birds to figure out their pattern and know for certain that mature gobblers are present. Watching birds helps me to know not only where to put the blind but also when to hunt it. I try to make sure my partner and I get in the blind before the birds arrive in the area—that is why watching the turkeys is so helpful. That can be before daylight if hunting birds close to the roost, or early to mid afternoon when hunting birds in the afternoon. Basically you want to set your blind up in a good location (that also means a good place to conceal it), set out some decoys, and wait. You need to position both hunters in the blind, so that either or both can get in position to make the shot when turkeys show up—I cannot emphasize this enough. Typically we will wait a little while for things to settle down, and then we start calling periodically, and waiting on birds to show. When I call from a blind, I hold the call up to an opening/window when calling, or stick my head up to the opening if using a mouth call. If you call from inside the blind, it sounds a little like the turkey is in a barrel and that is not very realistic. The keys to making this approach successful are good scouting and patterning of birds, proper location of the blind, hiding the blind if turkeys are spooky (as noted earlier, I always like to brush it in), and good planning for the shot. The hunters in the blind need to know in advance what to do, when, and how to shoot turkeys from the blind. Any hope of a double (getting two gobblers) is increased exponentially by a good plan for coordinating the shots when multiple gobblers show—who shoots what, the signal to shoot, etc. Don't assume anything—discuss it in advance.

Doubling up with Rookies. Buddy blind doubling is a particularly good tactic for hunting with a young and/or inexperienced hunter because they often have a tendency to move around too much and make other "rookie" mistakes. A blind can conceal a good bit of movement. Hunting inside the blind can also allow you to quietly provide the inexperienced hunter with verbal instructions as turkeys approach, and to coach them through getting the gun up, getting on target, and making the shot. It is not nearly so easy to communicate when sitting up against a tree with another hunter.

THE GOBBLER FIGHT

Simulating a gobbler fight appeals to another important instinct in gobblers, and that is the desire for dominance. Gobblers and hens both have a pecking order and mature gobblers will fight to establish and maintain that pecking order, to establish and maintain dominance. While serious injuries occur on occasion, most gobbler fights are just pushing and shoving, flogging with the wings, and lots of noise. They go at it chest to chest, with necks stretched out and heads up, jockeying for position such that it looks like they are trying to tie their necks in a knot. Each is jockeying for position to throw their legs up and use their spurs and inflict injury on the other gobbler. They can really flog the heck out of each other with their wings and they do actually spur each other, sometimes seriously. A gobbler fight is something to behold!

A vocalization produced before and during gobbler fights is the aggressive purr. When two mature gobblers are fighting, it is loud. If you ever hear the unmistakable sound of a gobbler fight, you won't forget it. Gobblers are like males of most species; when a fight is on, they want to be in on the action, if not to participate, then at least to watch. The gobbler fight tactic is an invitation to gobblers within earshot to come participate in or watch a gobbler fight. A single caller, skillful in the use of two calls at once, can simulate the sounds of a gobbler fight. Two hunters can do it even better! Basically you set up in a good area, be it in a blind or not, and you use two calls to make aggressive purrs in rapid succession-one call then the other, then the other, and I mean do it fast. You do it for maybe 15 to 30 seconds—it is not easy to keep it up for long because it takes a lot of energy and intense concentration to get it right. I use a diaphragm and a friction call (slate, aluminum, ceramic, or whatever) when I do it by myself and can do it pretty well. I pat my pant leg rapidly in between series of purrs to simulate the wing floggings part of a gobbler fight. If you have a call that will produce a realistic gobble, throwing in a few gobbles in rapid succession before or after the series can help complete the illusion of a gobbler confrontation. After the first series I listen for a response, but if I get none, I do another series then wait for a while before repeating it. If I hear a gobble, rather than repeat the fighting sounds, I wait a little to see what he is going to do. If multiple gobbles indicate to me that he has started in my direction from a distance, I may make a few yelps and clucks as he comes my way. It just depends on what he is doing. If a gobbler is really close when he gobbles in response to my gobbler fight, I just get my gun up and get ready. This tactic will sometimes bring them in on the run, so you should be ready. They may gobble as they approach, but they may just run to the fight without making a sound. If a bird gobbles, but does not seem to be coming in, I usually let out an aggressive series of hen yelps and maybe cut some and see what he does then. If nothing, I may gobble or repeat the fighting sequence. If he starts towards me, I play it by ear to work him on in. As noted, I sometimes will try the gobbler fight again, but it has been my experience that if he does not show interest in coming to you after the first series, another probably won't make much difference. He may be a lover rather than a fighter and have hens with him! What would you do in that situation if you were him?

I have watched a video of David Hale, of Knight and Hale Game Calls, using two push box calls to simulate the aggressive purrs of a gobbler fight. A fellow can use those two calls to make aggressive purrs without great difficulty because all you have to do is coordinate your two hands. David Hale makes it sound good. He highly recommends this tactic to entice gobblers that have hung up. Since his company sells push box calls, he obviously thinks they work best! I find calling with a mouth call and using a friction call with my hands to simulate the sounds of a gobbler fight to be a challenge. Coordinating my mouth, left hand, right hand, and my brain takes concentration. With a bit of practice, I got it down! I can do it well enough to fool a gobbler. I think that two skilled callers can reproduce the sounds of a gobbler fight better than one. Lance and I can produce one heck of a gobbler fight and have used it on occasion in conjunction with our noisy flock tactic, to add realism to our simulation of a turkey flock. Having watched numerous gobbler fights, I know what it sounds like, and that helps too. The Gobbler fight is a good tactic to try when other tactics are not working, especially late in the breeding season. I seldom start a hunt with the gobbler fight, but have used it on occasion to stir up a gobble where I could not raise a gobble any other way, and to entice a gobbler that hung up to come on in. It can and does work, but not every time, just like anything else.

To help you understand what a gobbler fight is like, I will tell you about the most memorable gobbler fight I ever witnessed. One year when we were down in Texas hunting Rios, we observed a gobbler fight like none I have ever seen. A bunch of Rios came off the roost and landed on a place we called the "runway." The turkeys would just pile into that open area at flydown from a nearby roost, then scatter into the mesquite country to spend the day feeding and such. Each morning there would be 20 or more gobblers in that roost area with a large number of hens. The roost was an area comprised of good sized trees (not common in mesquite country) behind a stock tank to which the birds headed to roost each evening. This particular morning, gobblers poured on to the runway as they usually did, but two gobblers got into a fight right off the bat. When they did, every other gobbler present ran to it with most jumping right in the middle of it. It looked like a whirlwind of gobblers with feathers flying, wings beating, gobblers jumping out, and gobblers jumping in. It resembled a goal line stand in a football game where all the linemen pile up on the line of scrimmage. Jakes and a few mature birds stood around to watch, but most joined in the ruckus. Before daylight, we had put Bubba (yes that is his real name), who needed one more gobbler to get his limit, in a mesquite blind I built by the runway the day before. He was about 25 yards from the gobbler fight. Lance and I were watching with binoculars from the cover of a popup blind about 100 yards away from Bubba and the fight. I never saw anything like it, before or since! As the fight started breaking up, gobblers came out of the pile one at a time, as if the whirlwind was throwing them out, and they headed straight in Bubba's direction. One got by him so fast he did not have a chance to shoot. He nailed the next, and the rest somewhat reluctantly gave up the gang fight and made a hasty exit. Bubba's bird had deep gashes of a half- inch or longer in his breast from fighting. They were not from the fight that morning, but instead were old injuries infected with gangrene. That was not the only such fight we witnessed, but was certainly the most spectacular. The sights and sounds of that fight are something I will never forget. We killed many Rios, with fight-related injuries to their breasts and legs, while hunting on that Texas ranch over the years. It seems to me that Rios must fight more than any of the other subspecies I have hunted. Perhaps that is due to the large number of mature gobblers that share common territory, and especially roost areas, in the open areas where we hunt Rios.

GOBBLING

Gobbling is more than just the mating call of a gobbler; it is a turkey hunting tactic. First let me say that gobbling can be a dangerous tactic to employ; it can get you shot! It is particularly dangerous in areas where other hunters are present, and more so when you don't know who is hunting around you. In short, this tactic must be used with great care. With gobbling, as with the gobbler fight, you are appealing to a gobbler's other instinct—dominance. When you use it with hen sounds, which I sometimes do, you are trying to make a gobbler jealous.

I have a friend that uses gobbling as a primary tactic for hunting turkeys. He sets out a jake decoy that he has repainted to make the head bright, blood red—that seems to excite approaching gobblers. His preference is to employ this tactic in food plots or other open areas like fields or prairie. He sets up close by and uses a gobbling tube to gobble periodically. Rob has killed Easterns and Rios using this tactic, so I know it works for him. Rob also introduced Tim and me to the Gobbler Loungers we now use to sit comfortably when hunting open ground where no backrest can be found. Since Rob employs this tactic in open areas, wherein setup spots with a good back rest are rare, the Gobbler Lounger allows him to hide, yet sit comfortably for long periods of time, as he waits on a gobbler.

Gobblers will sometimes respond to gobbling during stage IV of the breeding season when they might ignore hen calls. When I was a teenager, I called a late season long beard in from probably a half mile off by gobbling with my Lynch's World Champion Box call. I had learned to gobble with it pretty well—it was designed to gobble as well as produce hen sounds. That gobbler would say nothing when I yelped, but every time I gobbled, he would double and triple gobble. My dorm buddies from Mississippi State, Stan and Lou, were twins and very competitive. Both of them were carrying guns and I was not—I was the only one who could call. That old gobbler came right on in and one twin shot as soon as he saw the gobbler's head, and before the other twin and I could even see it. He missed! A fight nearly ensued with the one twin accusing the other of shooting too quickly just so he would not get a chance at the gobbler. It was ugly, but no one got shot, including the gobbler! Gobbling brought that gobbler a long ways to the gun, and I honestly don't recall him gobbling at a single yelp I made.

For me, gobbling is something I do when other tactics fail. Unlike Rob, I don't use it as a primary tactic. I use it when a bird hangs up, or won't respond to anything else. I tend to use gobbling when I other tactics fail. As noted, it can be particularly effective in stage IV of the breeding season when the hens are nearly done, and gobblers are about "gobbled out." While it is not always successful, it is a tactic that a turkey hunter should have in his bag of tricks for gobblers. It could be the trick that entices a smart old gobbler to come the distance. A word of caution is warranted here. This probably works best for mature birds who don't want an intruder in their area, and it can work when 2 year olds are hanging together in groups of 2 or more and they feel brave. A lone 2 year old might be spooked by gobbling. He might be scared of a butt whipping and take off in the opposite direction! It is also dangerous, so be careful when gobbling so that you don't get shot!

THE SILENT TREATMENT

I have mentioned the silent treatment in the context of a number of scenarios. I think it is important enough to deserve special emphasis. I have noted that the natural order of things is for the hen to go to the gobbler and that a turkey hunter essentially tries to get the gobbler to play another game, to come to a hen. Hen talk (calling) will sometimes entice a gobbler to come to the hunter. Notice that I say sometimes, which suggests that it does not happen every time or even most of the time. Calling can get a gobbler interested, and even get him to start in your direction. There are times when somewhere along the way he loses interest, encounters an obstacle, or gets with hens, and the game is over. Other times he comes to a point, maybe close but maybe not, and then decides to come no further. For any one of a number of reasons, forward progress stops! When he does that, and he is strutting and drumming in that spot, maybe gobbling now and then, he has decided that you, the hen that he hears but does not see, should come to him. I have mentioned numerous tactics that can break loose a hung-up gobbler and get him to come on into gun range. I have mentioned tactics like gobbling, the gobbler fight, aggressive calling, soft calling, scratching in the leaves, etc. All have worked for me at one time or the other, but the one thing that has worked for me more than anything else is the silent treatment. I believe that when that gobbler starts thinking that he has been rebuffed by a hen (ReeeeJECTED!), he responds like we men sometimes do; some combination of pride and curiosity drives us to find out why. For a prideful gobbler, that "typical" male response may just bring him the rest of the way into gun range. The silent treatment can entice a gobbler to come in and find out why the hen shut up.

When a gobbler is disinterested to begin with and rarely gobbles, the silent treatment is not likely to help. On the other hand, when a gobbler is fired up, but hangs up, this tactic can really work. You just shut up and wait with gun up and ready. It is a bit unnerving sitting there with gun up and nothing happening. If he keeps on gobbling, it is hard to stay silent. It is very tempting to call some more, thinking that if I can just say the right thing, he will come. When I was younger and had less patience, if something did not happen quickly, I just had to call again. As I have grown older and more patient, I have developed the self discipline to remain silent. It won't work every time, but I really do believe it is sometimes your best option for moving a bird that is hung up. Going silent is hard for most hunters to do, but it works. If you must do something during the quiet time, scratch in the leaves, but don't call!

This year I was hunting in Kansas and had the opportunity to watch a bird that was hung up like I described above. I was hunting a corn field and the bird hung up about 60 to 70 yards up the hill from me in the wide open. He had come in from a long way off, and when came over the hill to look, there was nothing but corn shucks and open space between him and me. I was backed into a plum thicket and well hidden, but I was pinned down with no way to move. I had no decoy out in front of me, or any way to get one set out without being seen. He gobbled, strutted, drummed, and gobbled over and over and over again. Occasionally he would come out of the strut and peck at some corn on the ground. When he would do that, I would yelp or cluck a time or two, then he would go back into his routine of strutting, drumming, and gobbling. It was a stalemate—a hang up!

I stopped calling, thinking he might get curious about the hen in the plum thicket that would not come to him, but after a while, he headed back over the hill the same way he came in. Note that the silent treatment did not work at first. I thought about sticking out a decoy, but was scared to risk it. I was afraid he might get the urge to peek over that hill one more time and bust me. I waited a few minutes then did some cutting and aggressive yelping. He gobbled again, and then came back over the hill to reassume the position. He did the same thing as before, gobbling, strutting, drumming, looking and staying put! Determined to try it again, I went silent! After about 5 minutes, he could not stand it anymore. He took a good, long look, perhaps he was not sure he could see what was down there, and he started down the hill toward my position. Thirty yards later I killed him! He was a two year old. If that had been a mature gobbler, I would bet a dollar to a dime that he would never have come over that hill the second time. It was a great hunt and illustrates several things. First, had I been set up closer to the crest of that hill, which I should have and could have been, the gobbler would have been in range when he topped the rise—my first mistake! Second, I should have taken the time to put a decoy out when I set up in that plum thicket, so when the bird was looking my way, he could see the hen making all that noise—my second mistake! Third, aggressive calling turned that bird around—done right! Last, but not least, the silent treatment employed a second time, brought him on into gun range—done right! A turkey hunter has to have plenty of tricks in his bag, and he must respond as the situation demands, mixing and matching tactics to fit the situation. I have to admit that when that bird was up the hill displaying for so long, I was sitting there thinking to myself can I kill him at that distance? It was tempting. When I was younger and short on patience, I would probably have taken the shot. Had I taken that long shot, a hunt that ended well, might have ended badly. Thank the Lord for finally giving me patience!

LEAVE HIM

A slight variation of going silent is imitating a hen that is leaving. With this trick, as with going silent, the intent is to make the gobbler feel rejected or curious. At times I go silent, and it does not work. If the gobbler is still hung up and doing his thing, I will usually next try to sound like a hen moving away. When using a diaphragm call, I very carefully turn my head to face dead away from the gobbler, or turn my head slightly and cup my hand to throw the sound behind me, then make some soft muffled yelps. With a friction call, box, or any call I use in my hands, I turn my body and use the call on the side of my body opposite the gobbler's direction. Basically, I want the gobbler to think the hen he has been hearing has given up on him and is leaving. I most often try this after going silent without success. Like all tactics, this one comes with no guarantee of success, but like all the others, it has worked for me and for others as well. It is just one more trick to try when a gobbler is hung up. When a gobbler hangs up on me, I try everything I know to get him to break away and come on in. I don't usually give up until he heads off away from me, or I run out of time and have to leave. I hate it when that happens, but remember what I said earlier; I often learn something from losing the battle that helps me emerge the victor in the next encounter. I don't like losing at anything!

CHAPTER 16
AFTER THE KILL

After you kill your gobbler, what do you do next? The best answer to that is it depends. When you hunt turkeys you must know the hunting regulations for the state where you are hunting. In some states where I hunt, the regulations require you to IMMEDIATELY tag your bird or fill out some area of your hunting license before moving the bird. Most states I hunt, including my own home state of Arkansas, have some form of tag that you must fill out, and normally it must be attached to the bird's leg. Typically, the tag must be filled out in pen, and sometimes a hole must be punched or a notch cut to record the date of kill. In some states you simply record information about the kill on your license and place nothing on the bird. I always carry some string and a pen in my turkey vest. The pen is for filling out tags/licenses, and the string is for attaching them to my gobbler if needed. Some states still require you take your bird to a checking station, record the kill on-line via a website, or use a call-in checking system. Arkansas uses an on-line game check now and it is more convenient for many hunters. In many states there is no such state requirement, but management areas within those states might require you to check your bird. If you hunt a management area, know the regulations for the management area. Those regulations, including bag limits, can vary from management area to management area within a state. Oklahoma has different bag limits for different counties. In short you should know the regulations where you plan to hunt and comply with them in every respect. Pleading ignorance will do you no good with most game wardens and judges!

PICTURES

Once you have done whatever the regulations require, you will probably want pictures of your trophy. I did carry my digital camera in my vest, but now keep it in my truck. Before digital, I carried a cheap throw away camera ($4 to $6, easy to use, and took pretty good pictures). Now, my smart phone takes pictures as most cell phones do, and I use it for my first pictures. I like to get a picture at the site of the kill if I can. If you have someone with you to take pictures of you and your trophy, that is all the better. When alone, I just prop my birds up in some way on rocks, or in the grass, to expose their beards and spread their wings and fans, and I take the pictures myself. I sometimes send pics to friends before I ever put the phone up—cool thing about smart phones. I usually try to get some good pictures of my birds with my good digital camera (takes high quality pictures) when I return to my truck, camp, home, or wherever I happen to be staying. I like to have someone take pictures of me with my birds stretched out to capture their beauty. I like to spread the wings out to each side, spread the fan, and make sure the beard is visible. If the spurs are exceptional, I will sometimes take a picture of them. I put my pictures on my website and my Facebook page, so I take upright (portrait) and sideways (landscape) pictures, so I have pictures for any desired use. I know some people don't care much about pictures, but for me it is important to preserve memories for myself and for my friends. Most of my hunting buddies also like to take pictures of their trophies.

Field shots: on left an Eastern, in the center the author with a Texas Rio, and on the right a couple of Nebraska Rios.

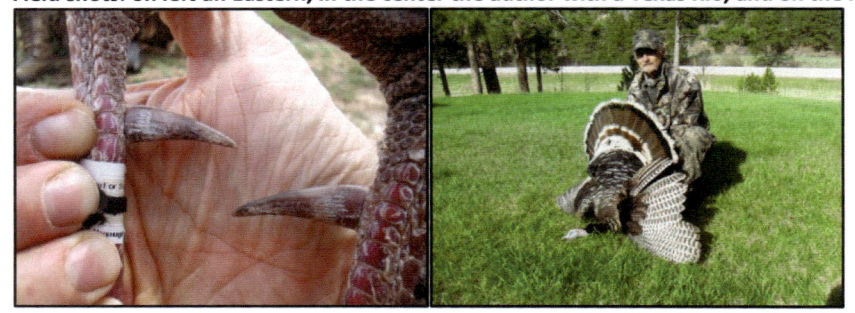

Back at the ranch: on left, the spurs off an old Texas Rio, and on right the author with a beautiful SD Merriam gobbler.

IN THE FIELD

If I am way out in the woods, or way up in the mountains and it is going to be a long time before I can completely clean (process) my bird, I usually do one of two things. One, I will field dress the bird, which means gutting him like a deer. Two, I will strip him and leave the carcass in the woods for the critters rather than hauling it out. Here again, you must know the regulations where you hunt. Some regulations require that you keep the bird in one piece, beard attached, until arriving at a check station, your home, or some "final destination." Some state regulations require you keep more than just the breast, and in those states throwing away the rest of the carcass can get you fined for wasting a game animal. You best know and obey the law! Simple field dressing won't violate the law in any state that I hunt, but it might in others. To field dress a gobbler, lay him on his back, part the feathers at the bottom of his breast (back end towards his butt), use a sharp knife to slit him from below the breast to the anus, then stick your hand in and pull out the guts. The guts will normally pull out in one wad with ease. Field dressing a bird is not a bad idea as it allows the bird's carcass to cool down more quickly and reduces the chance it will spoil before you get it out. Your bird is probably good for 6 to 8 hours this way in anything but extremely hot weather. Do not leave a field dressed bird in the sun. I always field dress my deer because I drag them out myself. It reduces the weight of the deer and makes the drag easy. I hardly ever field dress a turkey. It does not reduce the weight but a pound or two, and I usually stop hunting and get back to camp, home, or wherever, soon after I make the kill. In my view, field dressing is only necessary when it will be a long time before you can process your bird.

When I have a long walk ahead of me, and that may be an hour or more of rough walking in some places I hunt, I like to strip my bird. By stripping a bird, I mean removing the parts I keep as trophies (usually beard, fan, and lower legs with spurs), and the meat that I keep. I carry a couple of large ziplock bags in my vest primarily for this purpose. I carry disposable latex gloves for this task to keep my hands clean. When I strip a bird, I normally breast it, and take the upper thighs. This accounts for probably 80 to 90 percent of the meat on a turkey. If legal and I have a really long ways to walk out, I might keep only the breast. I put my trophies (beard, lower legs and fan) in one bag, the meat in the other, place them in my vest, and leave the remains for the coyotes and other critters. Again I want to emphasize that you need to know the regulations where you are hunting and comply with them to the letter.

REMOVING TROPHY PARTS

When you are done with pictures and back at your home or camp, you are ready to remove trophy parts from your bird. Most turkey hunters keep beard, spurs, fan, or all three. I will explain first how to remove each, and later how to preserve them.

To remove the beard, grasp it with your off hand, and pull it gently out from the breast until the skin at the base of it is protruding a little. With a sharp knife cut around the base of the beard. Try not to get more meat and skin than necessary, but also take care not to get so little that your beard will fall apart. It is not difficult. Err on the safe side and take a little more tissue, if you are unsure of yourself. You can always trim it off later if you intend to preserve it yourself. I will explain how later. If you intend to save the beard, fan, and feet for later delivery to a taxidermist, you can bag the beard with those parts after they are removed.

I recommend using a very sharp knife with an upswept blade for removing trophy parts and for processing the meat. I have done this with my Marine combat knife (a little big) and with a pen knife (a little small), but a medium sized knife works best. Most of my turkey hunting buddies use a medium size lock-back or fixed blade knife.

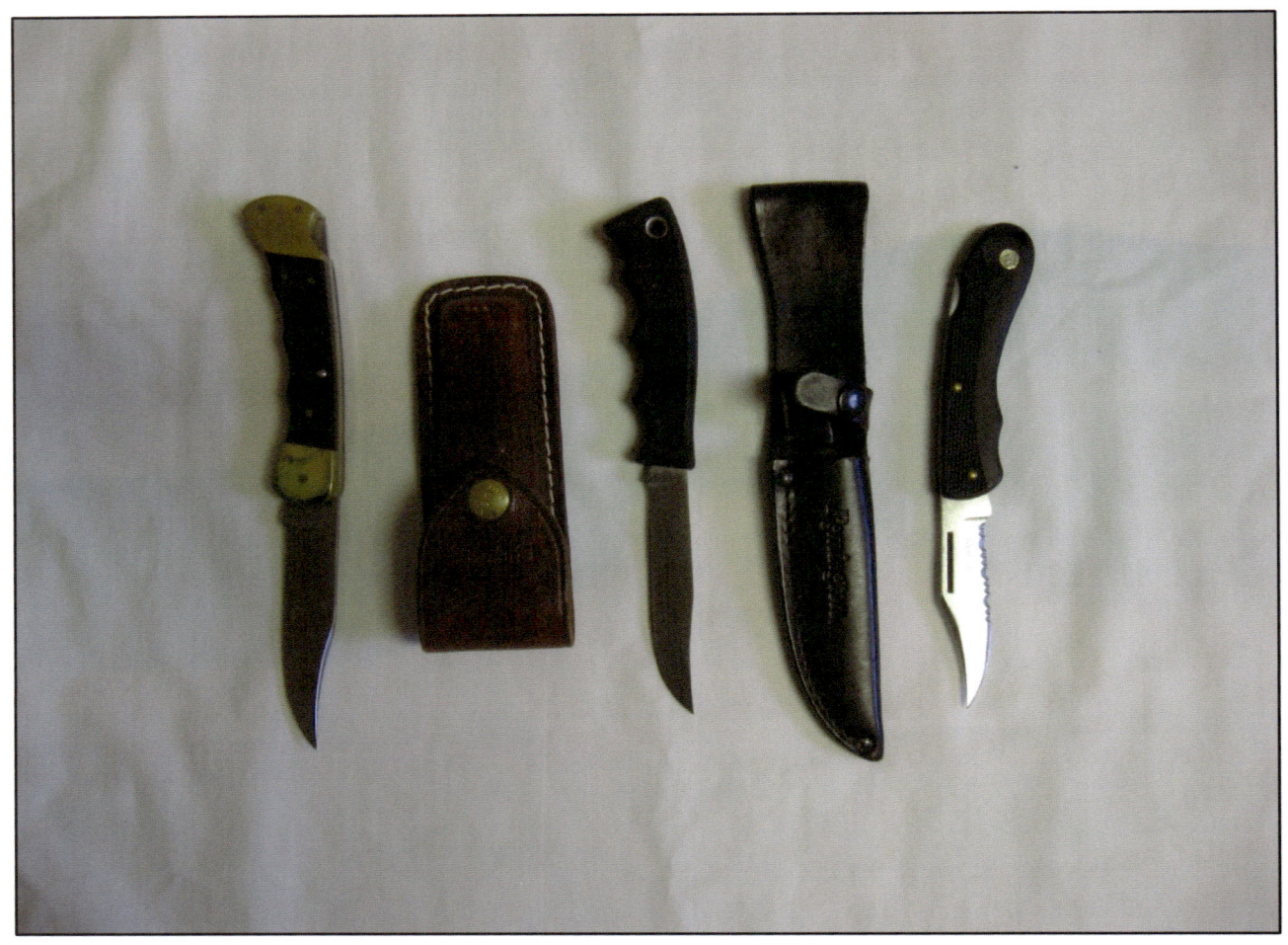

Good knives for cleaning a turkey: Buck folding hunter, Remington bird knife, and Puma folder with serrated edge.

To remove the fan, I prefer to turn my gobbler breast down/back up. With your gobbler in this position, close the fan, grab it in about the middle, and push it back gently towards the head so that it is at a 90 degree angle or more to the back. I am right handed, so I hold the fan with my left hand. With your free hand, push the secondary feathers below the fan (smaller black ones around 5 or 6 inches long—not the main fan feathers) down away from the fan (toward the anus) so you can see the base of the primary fan feathers (big ones), then use a sharp knife to cut down and away (toward the anus), not in one motion, but rather slicing skin and meat away from the fan as you move from side to side. You will start to see the little yellow, pocket like nodes that hold the fan feathers. Don't cut through them. If you push the fan gently toward the head as you do this, you can clearly see a vertebrae joint right below the fan. It is the base of the spine. If you pull up gently on the fan and tilt it more sharply towards the head, you should expose that joint as you cut away meat and skin. Starting below the fan, work your knife through it towards the back, but do so carefully so you do not cut through too quickly and through skin on the other side. I find it necessary to pry a little with my knife as I gently pull up on the fan and cut through the joint. When you get through the joint, you must be careful if you want to leave the colorful secondary feathers on top of the fan. I do! When through the joint, take your knife and carefully skin from one side of the fan itself to the other moving up the back a little ways, maybe 3 inches. This allows you to get a good portion of those colorful secondary fan feathers. The further you go up the back, the more of those feathers you will get with the fan—2 to 3 inches is usually far enough. If you will remove your fan in this manner, you can have a taxidermist put it on a plaque for you, or you can do it yourself. If you are going to take it to a taxidermist or dry it yourself later, fold it up and put it in a plastic bag (trash bags work well), then freeze it. It will keep well like this for several months. If you leave it too long, it will tend to dry out, making it tough to work with later. If you have no desire to keep your fan, I recommend you freeze it and donate it, and any others you don't want, to a local Boy Scout troop. That is what I do with the ones I don't keep. The Scouts make good use of the fans. Another reason for keeping the fans is to dry them fanned out for use on a gobbler decoy. I have gobbler decoys designed to accommodate a real fan. I am here to tell you that a real fan can make a gobbler decoy look so real it is dangerous!

Removing the lower portion of the legs is necessary to process a turkey in most any manner, and as a step in removing the spurs to keep and preserve them. To remove the lower portion of the legs with spurs intact, you can saw them off with a meat saw or hack saw, above or below the joint at the bottom of the drumstick, or you can cut through the joint with a knife. I generally cut through the joint. To do that, cut through the scaly skin around the front of the leg at the hinge point of the joint (thickest part), and cut all the way around the back of the leg, severing that very large tendon that runs up the back of the leg. You will likely have to cut that tendon a little below the joint. After making your cut through the skin all the way around the joint and severing the tendon, you can bend the leg backwards at the joint while twisting it gently (like hyper-extending your knee) and it will start to separate at the joint. Cut the ligaments and pry away the cartilage that holds it together as you work through it. If it is a little cantankerous, just twist it around one way and then the other while cutting and you can easily finish separating it from the drumstick. A friend of mine uses a large pruner, one with long handles like you use for pruning fruit trees, to cut the lower legs off right below the joint. It is quick and pretty clean! The lower legs can be placed in the bag with your fan and beard for temporary storage in the freezer.

PROCESSING THE TURKEY

With trophy parts removed, you are now ready to process your turkey for storage or for immediate cooking. There are a number of ways to do this. Generally, you can pick/pluck the bird, skin the bird, or strip the bird. Note I mentioned stripping a bird in the woods to make the trip out easy. As already noted, breasting out a gobbler and removing its thighs gets most of what is good table fare. This is, along with removing trophy parts, what I call stripping a bird. I often keep the wings for making wing bone calls, but I generally don't eat them. Before I describe in more detail the process of stripping a bird, I will describe the other two: picking/plucking a bird and skinning a bird.

Picking or plucking a bird is a lot of work (I will call it plucking for the remainder of the discussion), but if you want to cook the whole bird in the oven, smoke it, or fry it, this is probably the best way to dress it. This is without question the best way to prepare a bird if you intend to fry the thing whole. If you removed the guts when field dressing a bird, you should still check at some point and make sure you removed them all. If you did not field dress it, you can remove the guts before or after plucking. I think it is less messy after plucking. If you cold pluck a turkey, be prepared to spend a lot of time on it and to make a mess with all the feathers. Pluck it somewhere you can contain the feathers, like over a barrel, or do it in the woods where it does not matter about the feathery mess you leave. A turkey has lots of feathers, and some don't pull out easy (primary wing feathers for instance). While I don't recommend dry plucking, it can be done! Basically what you do is start pulling out feathers by the handful, and you continue to do so until there are none left on the bird. You need to be sure you get the fine pin feathers removed as well. They look like fine hairs, and are visible when the other feathers are removed. You can singe these off with a plumber's torch, or some similar device. That is a trick I learned from my duck hunting friends. If you don't singe them off, not to worry. Get all you can and eat the rest! You won't notice them at all if you fry the bird and will hardly notice them if the bird is cooked other ways. Note: your wife and kids will likely notice them, even if you don't.

If you want to make the plucking task much easier, scald your bird. Heat water in a large container until it is boiling. A turkey fryer works well for this task, as does an old cast iron wash pot, 55 gallon drum cut in two, or whatever. Obviously, the 55 gallon drum and wash pot require a heat source which can be a wood fire, gas burner, etc. If you use a turkey fryer (many people have these now days), make sure your pot is large enough. Regardless of what you use, you can cut the gas off or otherwise remove the heat source when your pot has reached a good boil. Be careful not to fill your container too full of water, because a big bird will displace quite a bit of water. Hold your bird by the head while lowering it carefully into the hot water. Be careful you don't scald yourself if water comes over the sides. A stick, broom handle, or such can be used to push the carcass down in the water. Leave it in the water for several minutes, then pull it up and see if the feathers slip easy. When you do this, I suggest you use a heavy glove to protect your hand from possible scalding as you grab a handful of feathers and pull. If the wad of feathers pulls out really easy, you are ready to pluck the bird. I plucked a lot of scalded birds, chickens mostly, over the years, and I can tell by the smell when it is ready. If it is not sufficiently scalded to make the feather's slip, put it back in and wait a little longer. When the bird is sufficiently scalded, remove it from the water and take it to where you will pluck it. It won't make as big a mess as dry plucking, but you will still have lots of feathers—they're just wet. You pluck a bird the same way after scalding as dry plucking. The difference is that it is easier to do because the feathers pull out easy, and it makes less mess. The downside is that it stinks worse! Be careful in scalding a bird because you can over do it. If you leave it too long, the skin cooks and gets soft. If that happens, skin pulls off when you are plucking it as opposed to feathers. If you do that, just go ahead and skin the bird. You can still eat it!

When your bird is plucked, cut the head off, gut it, making sure you get all the way up in the chest cavity and remove the heart and lungs. Also pull the esophagus and windpipe out of the neck. Wash the bird down well, inside and out, to remove all debris and feathers. You can save the giblets if you want to make gravy with them—very good. The giblets consist of the heart, liver and gizzard. You have to split the gizzard to remove the grit. It is shaped a bit like a large kidney, but it is very hard. Split it from the side opposite the tubes going in and out of it (cut from the smooth rounded side), from one end to the other. You will see the grit exposed as you cut into it. Spread it out and remove the grit and the inner lining of the gizzard that surrounds the grit. It pulls free of the gizzard itself—basically muscle—with little difficulty as it is very tough, thin, white-looking tissue. You should wash the giblets well, then wrap them in a piece of paper, put them in a bag, or whatever. I stick them back up in the now empty chest cavity right before storage. If you do that, don't forget to remove them before cooking. With the bird cleaned up well, it is ready for storage. I put it in a garbage bag or smaller trash bag, and wrap it tightly, making sure I get out all the air I can. I then put it in a second bag. If you are going to eat it right away, that is best. If you intend to freeze it, this packaging will protect the bird from freezer burn for only a short while (couple months). I recommend you eat it relatively soon. If you can package the bird with a vacuum sealer of some sort, it will keep longer without freezer burn. Vacuum packaging of such a large bird with the vacuum packaging equipment I have seen would be impossible, but perhaps capable equipment is available.

Skinning a bird is faster and easier than plucking. The downside is that if you intend to cook the whole bird, you lose the fat right under the skin and the skin itself—both the skin and fat enhance the flavor for a baked, smoked or whole-fried turkey. To skin a turkey, lay it on its back, and push back the feathers from the center of the breast. Start at the knot in the center of his chest, and with a sharp knife, slit it back to the anus and then, starting from the knot, slit it forward to the base of the neck. With that done, start peeling the skin outward and down toward the back all around the carcass. Push the legs out and down sharply, applying your weight. You should hear a pop as the legs become disjointed. This makes them lay flat on either side, thus making them easier to work around. Continue to peel (some cutting with a sharp knife can help) the skin down the sides to the legs. Now, slice through the skin you pushed down to the legs all the way to the top of the thigh, then out to the end of each leg. It will make them easier to skin. I cut the wing tips off (last joint where primary wing feathers start) before I start on the wings. There is not enough meat on the wing tip to worry with. Now you can peel the skin out and off the wings, or just cut the wings off in you don't intend to eat them. You might want to save them for wing bone calls. Basically, you continue cutting and pulling on the hide, turning the bird over and continuing on the back until the hide/skin is fully removed, in one piece or in pieces, it does not matter as long as you get it done. With the skin removed, you can gut the bird with ease. You should also pull the windpipe and esophagus free from the top of the breast, as well as the craw—craw looks like a bubble. Don't puncture the craw because it stinks. Gasses accumulate in it rather quickly because it usually contains seeds, grass, bugs, etc. When I am done cleaning and storing my bird, I sometimes open the craw to see what the bird was eating—part of scouting you might say! There is a lot of fatty tissue surrounding the craw in the center of the upper breast, so it helps to trim down each side of it with a sharp knife to remove most of it as well as the craw. After cleaning the bird well, you can store it in much the same way as described above for a plucked bird. You can also cut it up like you would a chicken for cooking or storage. If you do this, you can place pieces in zip-lock freezer bags, fill with water to displace the air, and freeze them. The parts frozen in water will keep very well for as long as a year. You can of course cook or store the whole bird.

A whole bird frozen with no skin is particularly prone to freezer burn, so you should probably eat it relatively quick.

Stripping a bird is my preferred way to dress a turkey, if it is not illegal where I am hunting. After removing the trophy parts, I start to process the bird exactly in the same manner as I do for skinning, right down to breaking down hip joint by pushing down on the legs and skinning out the legs. At this point (skin pushed off of breast and down to wings and thighs), no more skinning should be necessary, except perhaps a little tugging to remove what is left from the legs. I never put a hand on the bird's guts—they stay in the carcass as do the windpipe and esophagus. The craw remains attached as well. I cut around the craw to free it from the breast, so that when I remove the breast filets, it does not come with them. Again, be careful not to puncture it. Pull it gently away from the breast as you cut down both sides of it (See A and B on Illustration). With this done, and with the skin pushed back from the breast and down to the legs and wings, I remove the breast in two pieces—one from each side of the breast bone. I have hunting buddies that remove both pieces at once with the pulley bone and breast bone intact, but I see no reason to remove something I don't intend to eat—bone. I remove one filet at a time. With a very sharp knife, I cut from the knot in the center of the breast (See C on Illustration) back toward the end of the breast—the breast comes to a point where the abdominal cavity starts (D). The dashed lines connecting D and C on either side of the center of the breast bone show where I make cuts from the knot (C) back to the abdominal cavity (D). The dashed lines from (C) to each (E) show where I cut from the knot forward and down along the outside of the pulley bone on each side, to the base of the wings. You can see the very thin diameter pulley bone on both sides after cutting the craw away from it. I then slice away the breast filets as noted, one at a time. I try to stay as close to the bone as possible so not to waste any meat. I make short strokes with the tip of my knife in doing this (it's why I prefer an upswept blade), working all the way from the knot (C) to the abdominal cavity (D) while pulling the filet outward, freeing the filet from ribs that protect the internal organs. Then, while holding the portion of the filet I freed from the back of the carcass, I work my way forward from the knot (C) along the pulley bone pulling the filet away from the carcass as I slice my way toward the base of the wing (E). At this point the filet should pull right off, but if not, you can slice through the little bit of meat holding it, usually this will be at the base of the wing (E), to finish removing the filet from the carcass. The filets should pull off the carcass about where you see the dashed lines around the outside of the carcass in the Illustration. You will likely notice that a piece of the inside filet tends to pull away from the rest. I call this the "inner strap," but some call them "tenders," "tenderloins," etc. I go ahead and pull the inner strap off the filet at this point. Those inner straps have a tendon running the length of them, but they are good, so don't discard them. Repeat the process on the other side to remove the other breast filet.

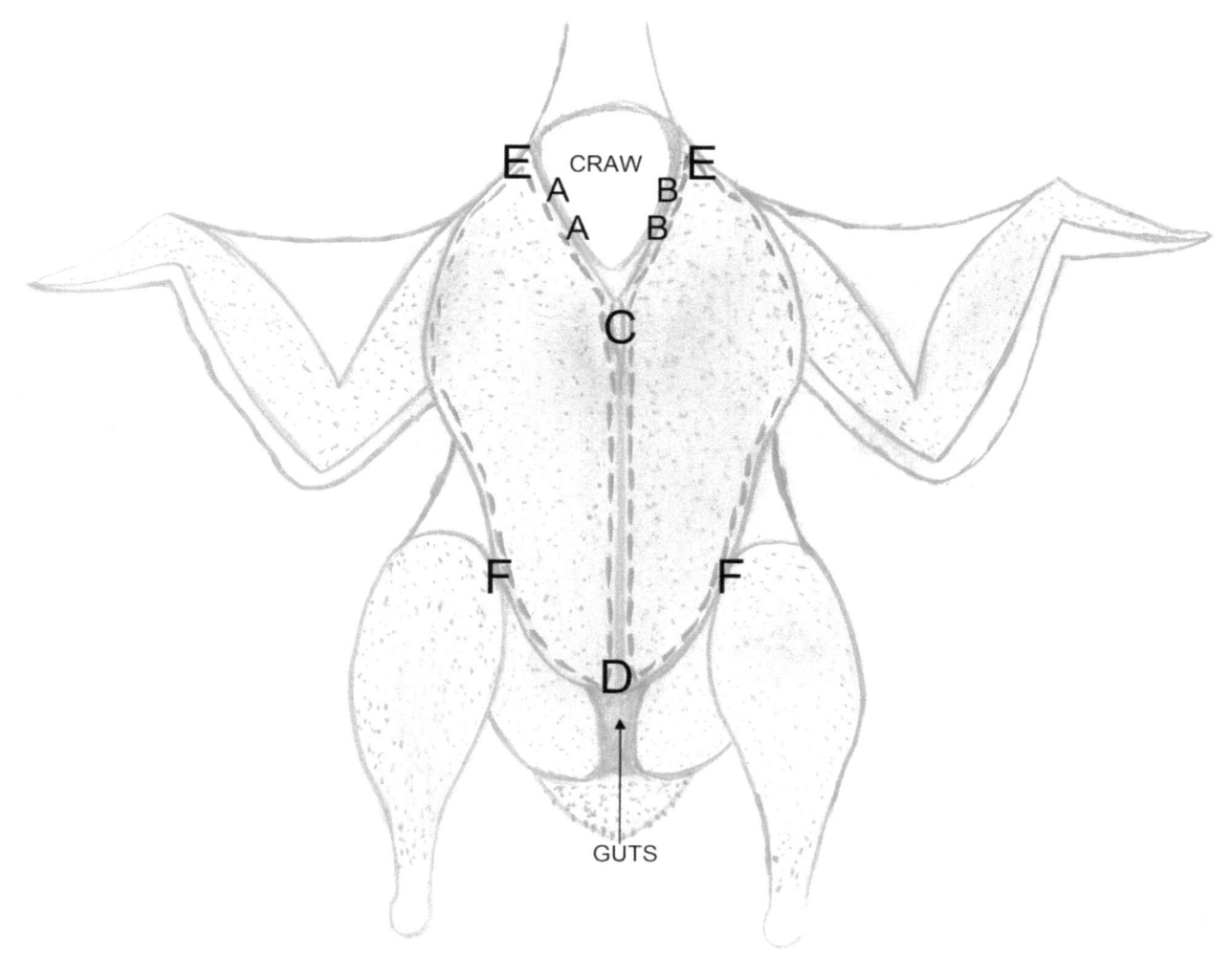

Illustration by Ottis Holland

Clean the filets up well before cooking or storing. For storage, I generally place each half of the breast in a separate quart size zip lock freezer bag. With the breasts in the bags, I fill each with water being careful to displace all air. You may need to squeeze each bag gently to move the breast around and get all the air out. With the water at the very top of each bag, seal them completely and place in the freezer, sitting upright so they won't leak. Breast filets frozen in this manner keep very well. Usually, I place the inner straps in the bags with the breast filets. If I am cleaning more than one turkey, I will sometimes put them all in one bag and freeze them in zip lock bags with water as described above. I can use a bag of 4 inner straps for soup, stew, turkey potpies, etc. I cut them in pieces and remove the tendon when cooking them that way.

If I intend to keep the legs, it is the thighs that I keep. In my opinion, the drumsticks would be better for playing a drum than for eating. Try eating them if you don't believe me! Removing the thighs is easy if you dislocated the legs as described. Pull the hide away from the thigh and down the drumstick. I pull it down to the drumstick, and stop there since I don't keep the drumsticks—my dogs usually get them. The thighs are easy to remove. There is a natural crease at the hip joint (F) that runs back to the abdominal cavity (D) and a little forward of (F). It is very obvious. Cut along that crease from front to back as you pull the whole leg away from the carcass. You may have to sever some ligaments surrounding the hip socket as you do this. The leg should pull free easily after you have cut all the way through to the top of the thigh. At this point, you can cut through to the joint between the thigh and drumstick, twisting as you to separate the two. When done, you should have the thigh in one hand and the drumstick in the other. Remove the thigh from the other side in a similar fashion. Now you can put the thighs away with bone in, or you can cut the thigh meat from the bone. To do that, simply make an incision the length of the thigh right along the bone. Then cut, pull and peel it off the length of the thigh to have a boneless thigh. I find the thigh meat to be good in turkey pot pies, soup, stew, etc. I like the taste of the dark meat, but it is generally tough and requires a long cook time to be tender. I do not cook thighs on the grill or fry them as I do breast filets. I freeze the thigh meat in zip lock freezer bags, using water to displace air and prevent freezer burn as described for freezing the breast filets.

If you are not going to eat the wings—they are very tough—and you are not going to keep them, then just leave them intact and discard with the carcass. If you want to save the wings for wing bone calls, sever them from the carcass at the joint and keep the first two sections. Remove the last section by holding the primary feathers (big ones on outward most section of wing), then severing it at the last joint (tip of the wing). You can dry that last section with the primary feathers and use a pair of them to make the sounds of wings beating at fly-down. Just place them up somewhere away from pests for a month or so and they will dry. That section is primarily feathers, gristle and bone, so there is really not much to spoil and stink. The remaining sections of wing should then be stripped of meat and feathers. I do this working from end to end, taking off large strips of meat with feathers attached. Strip away as much as you can, but since you are not eating the wing, you don't have to clean it up extremely well. You can freeze the wings for later use in making wing bone calls. I place the wings I save in a zip lock bag, and since I am not eating them, I don't worry about freezer burn. I usually add wings to the bag as I collect them until I fill the bag, or get ready to use them, whichever comes first!

THE SPURS

Some of my buddies dry the whole lower portion of the leg (cut off right below the joint) to preserve their trophy's spurs, some with feet spread, and others with feet closed. One buddy puts his in the freezer for a year or so to "freeze dry" them, then takes them out, air dries them for a while, sprays them with shellac, then sticks them on a shelf, hangs them below a fan, or whatever. I have preserved the whole lower leg, but dipped them in borax at the joint to coat them well, and then air dried them for a month or two. They might stink a little at first, but when good and dry, they pretty much lose the smell. One buddy just cuts the lower legs off, throws them on a shelf somewhere, and that's it. They eventually dry enough that they don't stink.

I now remove the spurs from the legs and save only the spurs. To do it, you can use a hack saw to cut through the leg right above the spur while holding it steady by the foot. Then, cut through right below the spur in like manner. Try to make your cuts square and allow maybe an eighth to a quarter of an inch on either side of the spur, so you don't get into the spur when you saw through the leg bone. I prefer to remove the skin and scaly tissue from the bone—gives them a cleaner look. To do this, a utility knife (razor knife) or very sharp, small pocket knife works well. Take the blade and cut around the base of the spur, not getting to close to the horny tissue. Cut all the way around the spur, then strip away the flesh and skin by cutting down and away from the spur itself. If you get too close to the horny tissue of the spur and leave too little tissue at the base, the horny tissue will pull away from the bone as it dries and slip off the bone. If that happens, just glue it back in place. I scrape and cut until I have a nice clean piece of bone with spur intact. Tendon runs along that portion of bone, so be sure you scrape it off as well and don't forget to remove the marrow from the bone. You can push a small stick, Q-tip, or something similar through the center of the leg bone to push out the marrow. When the spurs are good and clean, drop them in some borax (preferred) or salt for a week or so to dry them. Cover them completely with the borax or salt in a cup without a lid on it, or simply coat them well and lay them on a flat surface to dry. Allow them to dry at least a few days then spray them with shellac to preserve them. I string them on a piece of stiff wire or a coat hanger to allow me to hold them while I spray them good all the way around. You can display your spurs various ways. In about 2002 I started stringing each season's spurs on a leather loop for display on fans or elsewhere. They can be strung on a necklace, or used to adorn leather lanyards that hold wing bone calls. I use a black permanent marker and put the two letter state abbreviation and year on each like, "KS 09." There are many ways to preserve spurs. How you do it depends a lot on what you plan to do with them.

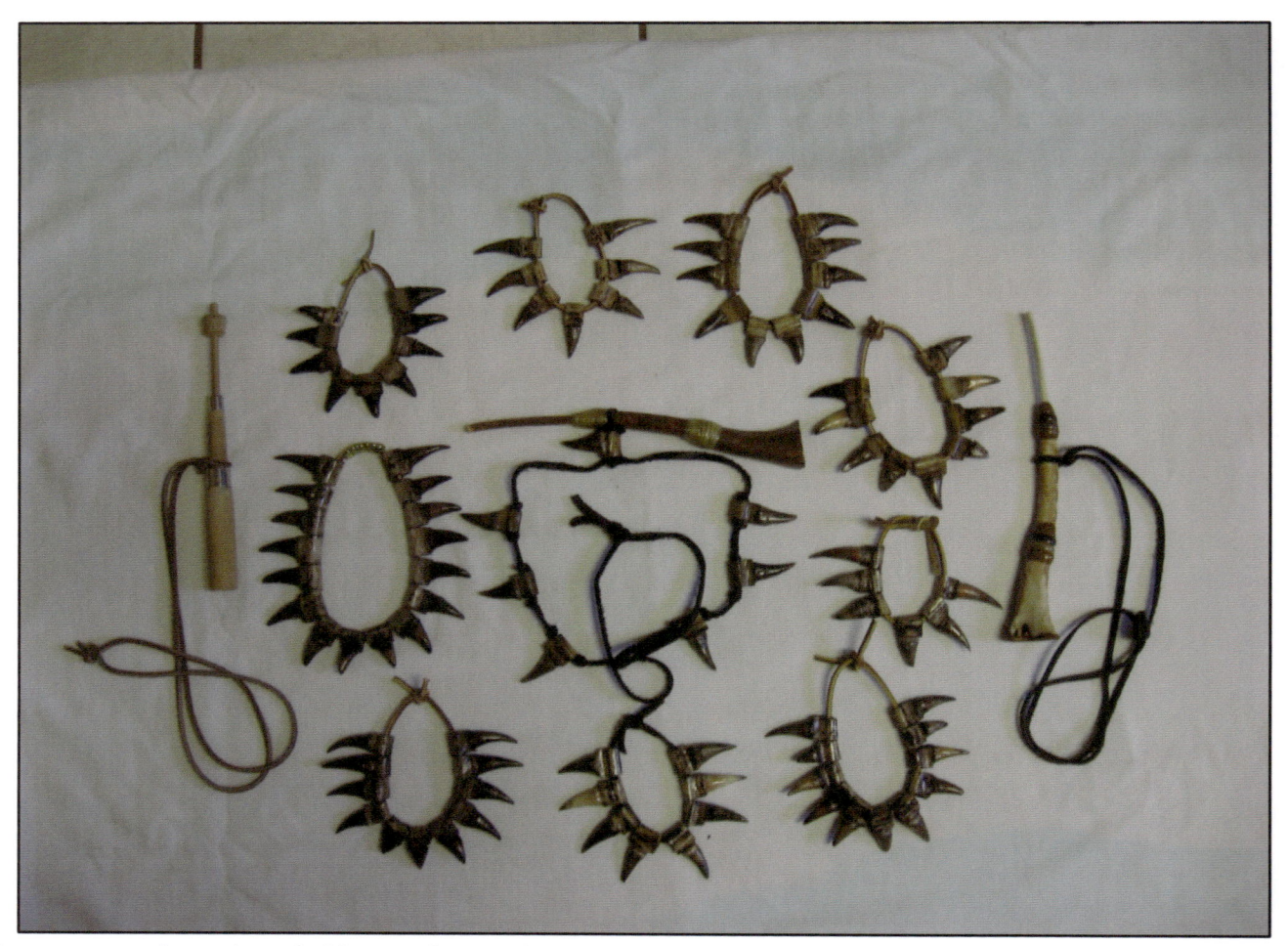

Here are my spur loops pictured with some of my wingbone calls. The call in the middle has spurs for decoration. I often dye my spurs with homemade walnut dye prior to shellacking them. It gives them a nice rich brown color like the middle call.

THE BEARD

To preserve a beard, I trim the excess meat from the fleshy end until little but skin and gristle remain to hold it together. I dip the fleshy end in borax and let it dry for a week or so. When dry, I tap it on something to remove the excess borax, and then spray the whole beard lightly with flat or semi-gloss shellac to preserve it. I tie a small piece of string at the base of the dried beard so I can hold it up and spray it lightly all the way around. I often hang it by that same string, so I use red string for this purpose. If you leave too much meat at the base and don't preserve your beard in some form or fashion, you may pick it up one day only to have it fall to pieces in your hand. I have beards that are probably 30 years old and still as good as new. My method of preserving them works!

Beards: many of my beards are displayed on this arrow. Some beards I use on fan displays. All of my turkey beards are sprayed with shellac to preserve them.

THE FAN

Preserving the fan is not particularly difficult. A properly dried fan can be displayed in many ways or you can use it on a gobbler decoy. To prepare your fan for drying, start by trimming as much of the meat as you can from the base of the fan. Use a sharp knife. A utility knife works well for this as well. Roll the skin on the top side of the fan back, and trim away as much meat as possible. When it is clean, it will have little red meat on it. It will be held together primarily by gristle (cartilage) and skin. With the skin still back, sprinkle it with borax on top, then turn it over and sprinkle the bottom as well. Work it in and sprinkle it again. This will preserve it, and keep insects off of it. You will need a piece of plywood, or something similar, as wide as the fan will spread or wider and a bit longer than the fan is tall. A little too long and wide is far better than too short and narrow. Cut two strips of cardboard about 1 and ½ or 2 inches wide. One should be about 12 inches long and the other about 18 inches long. You will need some small diameter nails to hold the cardboard strips in place—nails about two inches long. I use galvanized nails so they don't oxidize (rust). It is not really necessary if you use borax, but if you substitute salt, regular nails will rust. If the nails are too large in diameter, they will damage the feathers, so don't use big nails—4 penny nails work nicely for me. I also prefer to use nails with heads because finishing nails have no head and can pull through the cardboard.

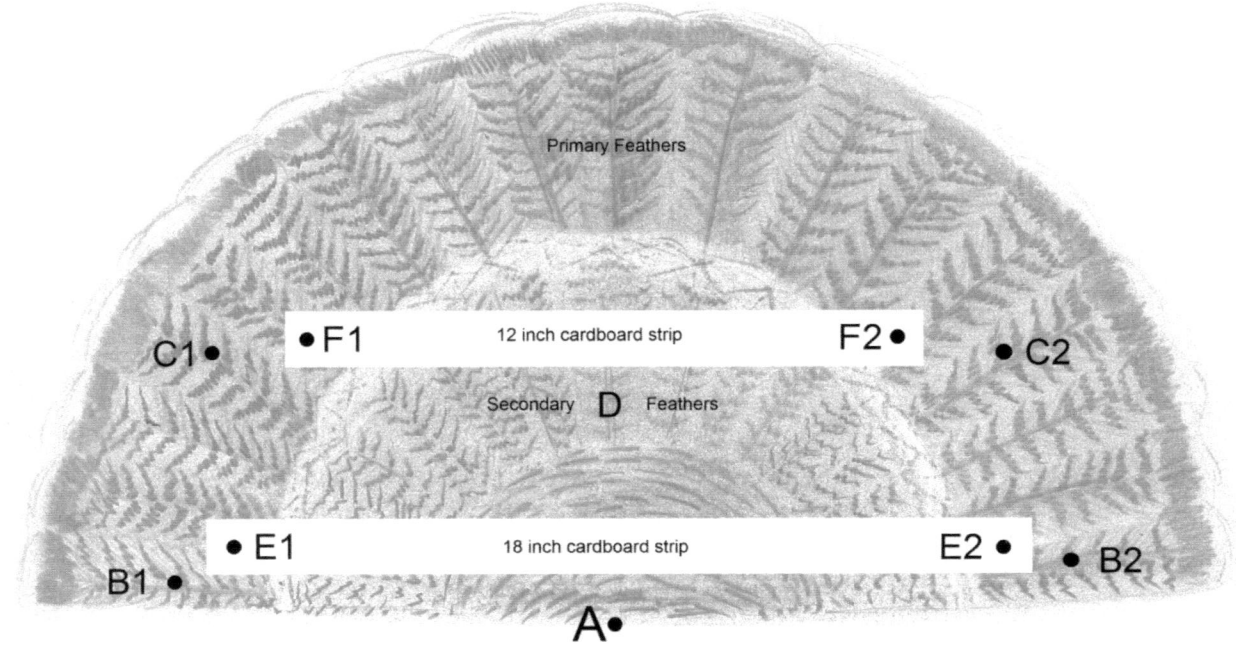

Illustration by Ottis Holland

To get started, place some borax on the board, bottom center, where the base of the tail will be positioned. Lay your fan down on the board with the front side up and the bottom portion of the tail in the borax. Tack a nail at the base of the tail (See A on illustration), so when you push the outside feathers down toward the bottom of the board to secure them, the bottom center stays in place. With the fan spread, tack a nail above the bottom feather, about 3 or 4 inches from the tip, on each side to hold the bottom of each side of the fan in place (see B1 and B2). You want the bottom nearly straight from side to side as illustrated. With each side secured, try to even out your feathers all the way around, putting them as best you can in the correct position for a fan spread out in full strut. I often place another nail about the 3rd feather up (see C1 and C2) on each side to keep the fan spread out. I usually remove these nails after tacking on the first cardboard strip. Next, you must make sure the secondary feathers are properly centered. Because they are attached by skin, you can move them easily. You want to get them centered in the big fan as best you possibly can, and spread out properly so they look like they did when the gobbler was alive (see D). You just have to use our judgment to properly position those secondary feathers. Not all fans that I have done are perfect. I have improved my method over time! The ones that did not come out so well, I use as fans on my decoys, or I gave them to the Boy Scouts—they generally separate the feathers to use them anyway. The cardboard strips you will now add will hold the secondary feathers in place, so before you nail the cardboard strip in place, make sure yet again that your feathers are properly positioned, both primary and secondary feathers. If your primary fan feathers are not staying in position, you can use more nails to hold them in place. I always do the nails in pairs to make sure the fan is symmetrical. Stick the nails in the cardboard strip before positioning it for nailing, because you will need one hand to hold the strip in position on the fan and the other hand to swing the hammer. Place the nails in the cardboard strip so they will be at or slightly beyond the tips of the secondary feathers, and not too close to the tips of the primary feathers. Lay the cardboard strip in position and spread your hand across it in the center of the fan with slight downward pressure to hold it securely in position. Tack a nail at one end of the cardboard strip, and then do the same with the other side (see E1 and E2). I place each nail at a slight angle—head slanted out toward end of primary feathers. This will keep the cardboard from sliding up the nails where it won't hold the feathers down firmly. You can move the feathers around a bit—you are mostly moving secondary feathers—at this point to make sure they are in place where they look natural. When you are good with the positioning of your feathers, put nails in the second strip, then place it across the fan covering the top portion of the secondary feathers to help hold both the primary and secondary feathers in place. Now tack that strip in place as you did the other, placing the nails out beyond the tips of the secondary feathers on the right and left (see F1 and F2). Do some final positioning of your feathers if necessary, sprinkle more borax on the base of your fan, and it is ready to dry.

Your fan should be placed somewhere safe where critters won't get it while it dries. I've put fans on the roof of my pump-house to dry them quickly in the summer sun (there are no cats around my house), but I brought them in each night. The hot sun of summer will generally dry a fan out well in 3 to 5 days. Most often, I leave my fans in my basement, which is closed in, cool, dry and free of varmints. I let fans dry in my basement for two to four weeks. Let your fan dry completely. If you take up the fan too quickly, the feathers will draw up and you will have a bowl shaped fan—not good. Give it plenty of time! Properly dried fans will be very hard and dry at the base. When the fan is dry, carefully remove the nails, shake it off and dust it off (I use another feather for this), then do with it what you will. I display mine in a number of different ways—I do them myself because I am too tight to pay someone to do it!

You can buy mounting kits to mount your fan, and make it look very nice. The cost of such kits generally runs somewhere between $10 and $20. One day I am going to do a video to show people how exactly I mount my fans—ONE DAY! When fans are dry, it is a good idea to spray them lightly with a pesticide, (like you use for bugs in a house—something non-toxic to humans is my preference). This will keep moths and bugs out of the fans. You really should spray them once every year or two to be safe. I have fans that are 20 years old, and they still look great. If you intend to store your fan for a while, spray it as described, and then slip it carefully into a garbage bag. Seal it up tightly with a tie, or whatever, and lay it flat. I have kept them stored safely in this manner for years. This is how I store the ones I use on my gobbler decoys.

118 • The Book on Turkey Hunting

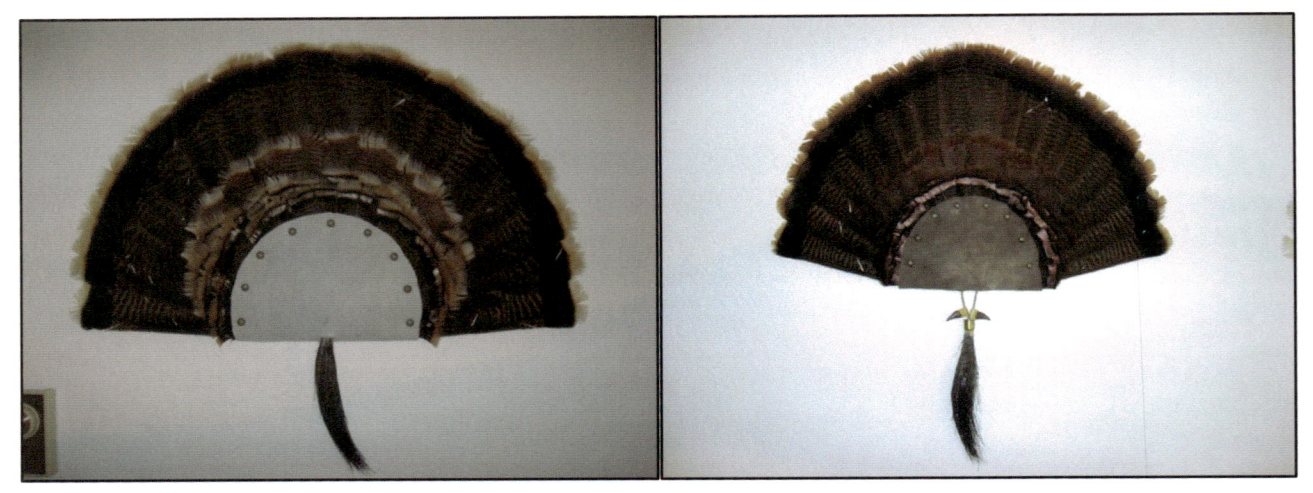

On the left is a Rio fan decorated with only a beard.
On the right, is an Eastern gobbler fan with beard slipped in shotgun shell brass and adorned with spurs.

Above is Merriam gobbler's fan with a spur loop for decoration. Note the beauty of the Merriam fan.

CHAPTER 17
TIPS ON RIO, MERRIAM, AND EASTERN GOBBLERS

When I made my first trip to Texas, I made little effort to learn about Rios before I went. I recall thinking that turkeys are turkeys, and I have hunted them all my life; therefore, I know how to hunt turkeys. I was quite surprised to see how different Rios in Texas were from the easterns I had hunted throughout the south. I killed three gobblers on my first trip to the Texas Mesquite country, but I learned that all turkeys are not the same. Because the Rios on the ranch I hunted were so numerous and seldom hunted, it was almost too easy and left me "over confident" in my turkey hunting ability. I experienced much frustration on my first trip to the Black Hills of South Dakota to take a Merriam gobbler and on my second trip as well. It was not until my third trip to the Black Hills that I finally killed a Merriam gobbler. I have killed a Merriam in the Black Hills every year since, but I had to adapt my hunting tactics to the turkeys—they were not going to adapt to me. I also had to adjust my hunting gear to the environment. Understanding the differences in the subspecies, terrain, food sources, and weather in different locations can impact your turkey hunting success. My observations herein are based on what we academics call anecdotal evidence. That means my conclusions are not supported by the results of carefully conducted scientific research. That said, the redneck in me tells me that "if it looks like a duck, walks like a duck, and quacks like a duck, it is probably a duck." Long story short, my observations are based largely on inductive reasoning and opinion, but they help me kill turkeys. Hopefully, some of my observations can help you do the same.

RIOS

Rios are in my view the most sociable subspecies of wild turkeys. It is not unusual to see flocks of Rios comprised of many gobblers and hens in the spring. In open country, which is the preferred habitat of Rios, I believe Rio gobblers and hens can hardly avoid coming in contact with other turkeys as they use scarce roosting sights and seek out food sources. I have, during my spring hunts in Texas, seen Rio flocks with 20 or more gobblers and numerous hens. I have seen spring flocks with many Rio gobblers and hens in Kansas and Oklahoma as well. That is not common behavior among the Eastern birds I hunt throughout the south. You might see many eastern gobblers together in flocks during winter, but not typically during breeding season. It may be because Rio gobblers tend to "share space," that they fight a lot.

While that might not exactly be "sociable," I think frequent Rio gobbler fights are likely a consequence of unavoidable gobbler interaction in the open areas they inhabit. Because Rio gobblers often travel in groups, I believe it increases the probability of doubles for an individual hunter (if legal) or for pairs of hunters. I have scored numerous doubles while hunting Rios.

Rios love to gobble during mating season and tend to do so more throughout the day than other subspecies that I have hunted. I have killed Rios at all times of day, and if you can get one to gobble, you have a chance to kill him, no matter what time of day. I also find that the Rios in areas I hunt respond well to loud, aggressive calling. Perhaps this is due to the open country they inhabit and how sound carries therein. Whatever the reason, I have good success screaming (calling loud) at Rio gobblers. I particularly enjoy hunting Rios because I enjoy aggressive calling and lots of gobbling. I noted earlier that the gobble of Rios will sometimes fool you. Mature Rios will sound like jakes more often than eastern or Merriam gobblers. It may just be the open country and indigenous flora making the gobbles sound muffled, but it is not my imagination—my hunting buddies have noticed this too!

Rios tend to cover a lot of ground during the day, perhaps traveling 5 miles or more to a food or water source. In Texas, the Rios that my buddies and I hunted at fly-down were not the same ones we hunted at ten, twelve, two, and four. Different turkeys moved through the areas we hunted during the course of the day. We had good success in Texas just waiting for the next bunch of turkeys to come through. I should note that feeders are legal and common in Texas. Feeders were scattered about on the ranch we hunted as were stock tanks, thus the birds had a reason to frequent the areas we hunted. Natural food and water sources have a similar effect on Rio movement in Texas and elsewhere. When Rios hit the ground in the morning, they tend to start moving quickly and cover some ground.

In Oklahoma, Nebraska, and Kansas the terrain and food sources are quite different from those where I hunt in Texas. In the locations where I hunt in those states, the Rios rely heavily on newly planted crops or grain, mostly corn and Milo (grain sorghum), that remains in the fields after the fall harvest—it's farm country. Rios in those places leave the roost and move quickly to the fields where they are feeding, so if you don't get your gobbler off the roost, you probably better plan on covering some ground to get to another position to hunt him, or other gobblers. I have hunted eastern gobblers that would fly down and stay in the vicinity of their roost for an hour or two, then never get more than 400 or 500 yards from it during the day. This is not the case for the typical Rio gobbler, so you need not expect to kill a bird you set up on at fly down in the same area two hours later. It probably won't happen! You have to be mobile and move as the turkeys move, using available cover to conceal your movement, or do as we do in Texas—wait for the next group to come through the area—but you best be on a food source or travel route.

In the open country of Oklahoma, Nebraska, and Kansas, you can often use hills and draws/coolies to conceal your movement as you circle around turkeys on the move in order to cut them off. You generally must move quickly, though, because they do! In Kansas, Oklahoma and Nebraska, when they get out in open fields, it can get tough, particularly in areas where they have been hunted hard. Educated Rio gobblers, those that have been hunted, seem to know that the middle of a large field offers safety, and they will stay out in those open areas, remaining unapproachable all day long. Either you get them before they reach their "safe zone," or when they leave it heading back to roost. They start to move toward the roost around an hour or two before dark where I hunt in Kansas, Oklahoma, and Nebraska. They may gobble some at this time of day, but from what I have observed, not a whole lot—at least not like they do in the Texas Mesquite country.

In the Mesquite country of Texas, Rios tend to start moving back in the general direction of their roost 2 or 3 hours before fly up, probably because they often end up so far from their roost during the day in search of food and water. They then hang out in the general vicinity (that means a half mile or so in Texas) of the roost area until fly up. I have observed Rios doing the same thing in Oklahoma, but the Oklahoma Rios tended to get even closer to roost areas where they would hang out and strut for the last hour or so before fly up. If you will scout the roost areas where you hunt Rios and learn their pattern in the late afternoon, you may just get in on some good late afternoon action. In the Texas mesquite country, Rios tend also to gobble a lot more at this time of day than other subspecies that I have hunted, and even more than Rios I have hunted elsewhere. That can make afternoon hunting down in Texas as exciting as early morning hunting. I have worked Rios down in Texas that gobbled their heads off in the late afternoon.

During the heat of the day, the Rio gobblers in Texas as well as those I have hunted elsewhere, tend to seek shelter from the sun in the middle of the day, often in the same place day after day. Many times I have seen them in the same shady spot over and over, about the same time of day. In Texas where I hunted, I often saw turkeys resting under larger Mesquite trees that offered good shade, perhaps near a stock tank. In Oklahoma and Kansas, it was typically locust trees or other similar shade trees that offered the shade Rios sought out for their Siesta. It may be a small clump of trees in the middle or near the edge of a field in farm country. Little "islands" of trees in the middle of fields that Rios are using are good bets. Many times I saw them holed up in the shade in such areas when I was hunting in Kansas and Nebraska. Whatever the case, if you can find these shady mid-day hangouts, and can approach them undetected, you may have a chance to take a Rio gobbler. Be forewarned though, because Rio gobblers seem to be good at finding shady spots that you simply cannot approach without being busted. Because gobblers and hens stay very still when resting, and because they sometimes squat as they rest, they can be very hard to see. Binoculars can be a big help in examining likely mid-day hangouts!

The Rios I have hunted nearly everywhere tended to roost in the same general areas each day. So, once you pinpoint a roosting area, you can generally expect the turkeys to roost in the same area each day. It may not be in the same tree, but rather the same general area. The scarcity of good roost areas in the open country Rios typically inhabit likely contributes to this behavior.

Rios tend to not be quite so spooked by movement as the easterns I am accustomed to hunting in the south. I think it is probably because there is constant motion in the Rios' environment associated with wind, livestock, other wild critters, and farm work. I am not saying that Rios are stupid, but I have gotten away with much more movement hunting Rios than I have with easterns, like moving my gun into position for a shot. Seems most easterns I hunt will haul butt at the slightest movement, and I mean as little as moving your trigger finger or blinking an eye.

In the places where I hunt Rios, the weather can be very hot, very cold, or anything in between. My buddies and I nearly froze on our first trip to Texas because we expected it to be hot. It was hot in the afternoons, but not early in the morning and at night early in turkey season. Throughout the Rio Grande range the climate is relatively dry so it can be cold in the mornings and hot in the afternoons; therefore, you need appropriate clothing and gear for it. I recommend having very light clothing, a light weight turkey vest or a fanny pack, and cool footwear appropriate for hot afternoon hunting, and I recommend taking clothes that allow you to dress in layers to stay warm in the morning and to adjust during the day by removing layers as it warms up. Rain is a fairly common occurrence in Kansas and Nebraska during the spring, so rain gear is essential if you hope to stay afield hunting and remain comfortable. A good blind also helps you remain comfortable in inclement weather. Where rattlesnakes are present—they are numerous in west Texas—I wear snake boots. Knee height rubber boots are helpful in Kansas and Nebraska because the grass is quite tall and dew is often heavy in the early morning. Your feet will get very wet without waterproof boots.

Because in open Rio country you often have to set up in places without a good tree for a back-rest, a low rise camo seat with a back on it is helpful. It will allow you to sit comfortably for a long time, and it will give you a little extra elevation to allow you to shoot over tall grass and weeds. A simple folding seat with no back is the next best thing. In Texas, my folding seat helped me keep from getting thorns in my butt. Nearly everything in west Texas has stickers or thorns on it. Mesquite thorns can cause a nasty infection, so you sure don't want one to stick you in the butt, or anywhere else for that matter! Locust thorns are not much better and they are abundant where I hunt in Oklahoma. For your information, Mesquite thorns and honey locust thorns can poke right through all but the thickest padded seats that come with most turkey vests.

MERRIAMS

The Merriams I have hunted are not as different from easterns as are the Rios that I have hunted. I must acknowledge that most of my Merriam hunting has been on public land in the Black Hills of South Dakota or in Nebraska. Public land turkeys from any subspecies are typically spookier because they are subjected to a lot of hunting pressure. I have also taken Merriam gobblers in the extreme northwest corner of Kansas (they have migrated over there from Colorado), and on private land in northwest Nebraska where they are not so spooky.

I find that Merriams in places I hunt, like Rios, often travel far and fast from their roost, but not typically in the large groups fairly common with Rios. I did hunt on some private land in Nebraska where the Merriams were in a very large flock, but I did not observe the frequent gobbler fights I witnessed with Rios, nor did the flocked-up Merriams gobble as much as Rios. On that ranch in Nebraska, there was essentially one place for the turkeys to roost, and all of the Merriams in the area roosted there in the only trees available. That may have accounted for them starting the day in a large flock. Those Merriams did break into smaller groups as the day progressed and most moved pretty far from their roost.

Merriams seem to gobble very well on the roost like easterns and Rios, but like easterns, they tend to gobble much less frequently once they hit the ground. The Merriam gobblers that I have hunted tended to gobble intermittently once they hit the ground, tapering off more and more as the morning progressed, much the same as eastern gobblers. I believe they do so to gather hens in much the same way as easterns do, and as they gather their hens and get busy breeding them, they gobble less. As already noted, Merriam gobblers seem to cover a lot of territory once they leave the roost. In the rough and rugged Black Hills, they likely have to do so to find sufficient food and to gather hens because the hens are typically scattered about the area. Turkeys can roost about anywhere in the vast wooded slopes of the Black Hills, so the Merriam gobblers there tend not to roost together in large numbers during the spring turkey season. I observed similar Merriam behavior in the rugged Pine Ridge area of the Nebraska National Forest where trees were abundant.

I have found that Merriams, while they have far more choice of roosting areas in places like the Black Hills, tend to routinely roost in the same general area, and even in the same tree. I think they are more prone to roost in the same tree than any of the three subspecies I hunt. I have found roost trees with enough droppings beneath to fertilize a garden. It is likely due in part to the harshness of the elements in Merriam country. A good roost site might be favored because it offers protection, not only from the elements, but also from the large predators in those areas—mountain lions are common in the Black Hills. Finding a Merriam gobbler's roost site, and his favorite roost tree, can put the odds in your favor when you hunt him. I have seen them pitch down-hill and up at fly-down, so knowing where exactly to set up on a Merriam gobbler, even if you find his roost, will likely involve some trial and error. Merriam gobblers do seem to like to pitch onto their roost from an elevated position. I have seen them do it many times.

Merriams I hunt in the Black hills and in the Pine Ridge area of northwest Nebraska will come a long way to the call. Any gobbler from any subspecies will do that on occasion, but if I can hear a Merriam when hunting those rugged areas, I figure I am close enough to set up and call to him, even if he is way off. During spring mating season, I have seen Merriam gobblers travel a very long way—a half mile or more—in response to my calling. I typically try to get much closer before setting up and calling to eastern gobblers and Rios in the places I hunt.

Merriams will often let you know where they are roosting by gobbling on occasion as they head toward their roost, and also when they fly up in the late evening, either on their own or in response to a locator call. I almost always use a coyote call to "roost em." Merriam gobblers are typically very willing to gobble at that call. Roosting a bird gives a hunter an advantage, especially in a vast area like the Black Hills, because he knows where the gobbler is located and has plenty of time to think about where to set up the next morning for the hunt.

I find mountain Merriams very unwilling to come down hill to a call, especially when they are fairly close. Any Gobbler will exhibit such behavior at times, but I find it to be particularly true of Merriams, especially in the rugged Black Hills of South Dakota. I believe it is very important to move to the same elevation of a gobbling Merriam to increase your chances of killing him. I tried many times to coax a Merriam gobbler to come down from a rough, rocky hillside above me, and almost never succeeded. Long story short, if he is up high, go up there with him if you want to kill him. Note also that the Black Hills in particular are very open and covered primarily with Ponderosa pines, so you have to be careful to pick a line of approach that will conceal your movement as you slip around on a gobbler. If he sees you coming his way, the game is over! The open terrain may also be why Merriam gobblers typically refuse to come down hill. Since most of the time they can see well from their high vantage point, they expect to see a hen. If they do not, they hold their position and wait until they do!

Merriam hens and gobblers look more alike to me than any of the other turkey subspecies. The neck feathers of Merriam gobblers tend to be thicker and run further up their necks than is typical for other subspecies, probably an adaptation to the harsh winter conditions where they normally live. That makes them look more like a hen; furthermore, the color of Merriam gobblers and hens is very similar. Both are very dark in color. When you see them together, hens and gobblers, size is a good clue as to which is which, but when you see gobblers by themselves, particularly in dim light and when they are not displaying, it can be hard to make a positive ID—to know you are looking at a gobbler and not a hen. Making matters worse, Merriam gobbler beards are often spindly or broken off where the winters are harsh. I have let gobblers get away from me because I was just not sure of the sex of the bird, only to recognize my mistake when the bird was out of gun range. I recommend you be sure to carry some good binoculars with you when you hunt Merriams in the mountains.

Merriams often don't skedaddle as if "shot out of a cannon" when they are spooked. I have seen mature gobblers just walk off babbling turkey small talk—a "peeping" sound like baby chicks make— when I walked up on them and spooked them. I am not sure why they do that, but the behavior is not limited to gobblers. I have seen hens do it as well. Since I was most accustomed to easterns that haul butt when spooked, I was somewhat surprised to see Merriams behave this way when I first started hunting in the Black Hills. A Merriam gobbler won't always do this, so don't count on it. Be thankful if it does and gives you a shot opportunity!

Springtime can be very cold in the mountainous range of the Merriam turkey, so be prepared and dress for it. Snow is not uncommon, so clothing and boots that will keep you warm and dry are advised. Make sure, also, that your equipment is appropriately conditioned for cold weather. I never considered the possibility of my turkey gun freezing up, but it happened to me in the Black Hills one cold morning in about 6 inches of snow and sub-freezing temperatures. I called a nice Merriam gobbler off his roost to about 20 yards. It was a perfect shot opportunity. I pulled the trigger and nothing! I thought there was something wrong with my safety, so I clicked in on and off pulled the trigger again. Still nothing! When I looked up, the gobbler was gone. I figured out later that my firing pin was frozen in place because of water that had remained in my 870 from the previous day's hunt. I thought it had dried out over night because I left it by the heater, but not so. I know now to make sure that I thoroughly dry my gun out the night before my hunt, and I keep the receiver portion of my gun tucked under my arm pit so that it won't freeze. Excess grease in your action can cause similar problems if it stiffens with the cold temps, so be sure you take proper steps to prevent it. Trekking up and down rugged mountains in Merriam turkey habitat can be rough on your feet. Good comfortable boots, with soles that provide good traction, are important and so too is good ankle support. A sprained ankle can put a damper on your hunt and can be dangerous when hunting "off the beaten path." I also consider water-proofing a must for my boots!

I recommend a folding seat for hunting Merriams or other turkeys in mountainous terrain such as the Black Hills, and in particular, one with adjustable legs. A seat like that allows you to sit comfortably on even a steep hillside. My Buddy Tim and I have set up on Merriam gobblers in places so steep that we could not keep from sliding down hill. Without our folding seats with adjustable legs, we simply would not be able to set up in such places. I used the same folding stool in the Texas Mesquite country and in Oklahoma where I was hunting Rios.

EASTERNS

I spent 37+ years hunting eastern turkeys before I ever made a call to a Rio or a Merriam, so I am most familiar with eastern turkey behavior. I could write a book about only easterns, and may do so some day. Easterns are more widespread than any other subspecies (inhabit every state east of the Mississippi River and then some), and I suspect that many more hunters hunt easterns than any of the other subspecies.

One generalization I can make about easterns is that they are spooky as can be in most places I hunt. The slightest movement or sound can send them on their way in a flash. Sometimes they make their exit on foot and sometimes they fly. They can run as fast as a horse, and as big as they are, they get up and go like a quail when they fly—very, very fast. Any of the subspecies can make a hasty exit, but it seems that easterns are always poised for it and do it more readily than other subspecies.

Easterns tend not to travel as far during the day in the places I hunt as do Rios and Merriams, and I believe it is simply because they don't have to travel far to find food and water in most habitat where they are found. I know for a fact that turkeys on my place in Arkansas will often hang out on no more than 20 acres from fly-down to fly-up. They have food, water, open ground, and cover in that small area, so they don't really need to travel far. This won't necessarily be the case everywhere you find easterns, but throughout most of the south, food is relatively abundant and so is water, so this behavior is fairly common for eastern turkeys in the south (Alabama, Arkansas, Georgia, Mississippi, Kentucky, Tennessee, Mississippi, etc.). Because eastern gobblers often don't travel as far during the course of the day, you can sometimes hunt an eastern gobbler in the same general area all day long.

Easterns like to roost near, and even over water. I once heard Ben Lee say that they like to roost where "they can hear their droppings hit the water." I have seen eastern gobblers roost around beaver ponds, creeks, rivers, lakes etc. Eastern gobblers seem to prefer such roost sites in the springtime when available. I have large pines on the back of my place in Central Arkansas and a creek bottom running through it. I find that in the early season, while it can still be quite cool, my eastern gobblers will roost in the pines up in the hills behind my home, perhaps because pines give them more protection from late frosts and from the cold winds of early spring. As it warms up, the gobblers move down into the creek bottom to roost and roost in the bottom for the rest of the season. I have observed this behavior in Mississippi, Alabama, Georgia, and Arkansas, where eastern gobblers favor roost sites in pines early, then near water during the remainder of spring turkey season. Rios and Merriams in the west also roost around water at times, but it seems to me that for them, it is simply because that is where the only trees are located. In much of the eastern wild turkey's range, trees for roosting are abundant so gobblers can roost about anywhere; however, when good roosting sites in proximity to water are available, eastern gobblers just seem to prefer them.

In the Ozark Mountains where I hunt, it seems that the eastern gobblers like to roost on the slopes just above or below benches, or near the peak but seldom right on the top. Merriams seem to do essentially the same in the Black Hills where I hunt, but will actually roost right on the peak. In these mountain locations, gobblers seem inclined to pitch onto their roost from an elevated position, probably because it takes less effort. When they fly down, they tend to sail into an open area, whether it is above or below them. I have seen eastern gobblers sail half-way down the side of a mountain before landing, something I have seen Merriams do as well in the Black Hills. I have also seen gobblers flutter straight down to the ground from such roost sites, landing right below the roost tree. This behavior, seemingly unpredictable fly down patterns, makes picking a set-up a bit more difficult in the mountains. Around a beaver pond, lake or river, it seems that the direction of fly-down is generally more predictable. An eastern gobbler will tend most often to fly down on the same side of any fairly large body of water as he roosted. Understand, however, that there is hardly anything absolutely certain about eastern gobblers' fly-down behavior, even the time at which they fly down.

I have observed easterns staying on the roost late in the morning more often than I have seen Rios and Merriams do so. Some eastern gobblers just seem to prefer hanging out on their roost longer. Some smart old eastern gobblers do it because they won't fly down until they see hens under their tree. I have hunted birds like that, as I noted in this book. If you call too much to a smart old eastern gobbler, that might also encourage him to stay on the roost longer. I have observed that behavior numerous times with eastern gobblers. It is why I warn against calling too much to a gobbler still on the roost. It is noteworthy that bad weather will keep turkeys of any subspecies on the roost later. For instance, I have seen Merriam gobblers stay on the roost late when it was snowing hard.

Mature eastern gobblers seem quite intolerant of each other during the breeding season. I believe this to be the reason why I have seldom observed eastern turkey flocks with numerous gobblers present, particularly in Stage II of the breeding season and beyond. An eastern gobbler seems to prefer to gather his harem, then to keep his distance from the competition. I have watched mature eastern gobblers with harems run other gobblers off, and I have watched them stay between their hens and other gobblers that were present. If another gobbler does accompany a dominant eastern gobbler and his harem, that subordinate gobbler typically won't be doing any breeding. Two year old eastern gobblers with no hens will tend to run together in flocks during spring as will jakes. Mature easterns are just not inclined to tolerate the presence of other mature gobblers during the breeding season, quite unlike Rio gobblers in the Midwest.

A word about jakes seems warranted at this point. Jakes of all subspecies can band together in large flocks in spring and harass mature gobblers and hens. I have seen such jake flocks terrorize mature gobblers in Texas, so much so that it was hard to get a mature gobbler to respond to a call. If they did, they were mobbed by jakes. In eastern habitat, I have observed that an abundance of these large jake flocks can cause mature birds to go "hush mouth," refusing to gobble and give away the location of their harem. In either case, large jake flocks can be a nuisance for turkey hunters as most turkey hunters are not out to shoot jakes.

Many of the things I said about equipment for Rios and Merriams can apply to easterns. Easterns inhabit terrain ranging from the Cypress swamps of the deep south, to the rugged Catskill Mountains of New York state, over to the upper Michigan Peninsula, then down to the open croplands of Iowa, the eastern Dakotas, and eastern Nebraska, Kansas, Oklahoma and Texas. Terrain, food sources, weather, and hunting conditions vary greatly over that broad range. One thing I have not mentioned is swamps and bugs. The south is full of swamps and that means water, snakes, mosquitoes, and even alligators. You must be prepared to deal with them, so I recommend proper foot gear, effective insect repellent, and watching your step! Comfortable boots that will allow you to wade across creeks or through sloughs, yet provide protection from snake bite are a must in my view. Cottonmouths, Eastern Diamondbacks, Timber Rattlers, Copperheads and Coral snakes can be found in the south. Any or all can be found in parts of the south where I hunt easterns. Good quality, knee-high, waterproof, snake boots are in my view essential hunting equipment in the deep-south. Some of my friends opt to use snug fitting, knee-high, rubber-boots like the ones that LaCrosse makes. Most of those guys are coonasses and they ain't scared of snakes or "gators"! Good insect repellent is also a must in the south, and while the new thermal cells work well for mosquitoes and gnats, they don't help much with ticks. A good spay-on repellent, with Deet (can use it on you) or Permethrin (for use only on clothing and gear but protects for up to 2 weeks), is effective on ticks. I think Arkansas is the tick capital of the world, so a good tick repellent is a must for me when I hunt around my home.

Not all wild turkeys are the same; furthermore, terrain, weather, and available food sources vary greatly over the ranges of the various subspecies. If you hunt them all, you will undoubtedly observe differences in turkey behavior. I am not sure how much of the behavior can be attributed to the genetics of the subspecies, or how much the behavior simply reflects adaptation to their environment. Either way, recognizing and understanding the differences in turkey behavior, habitat, and hunting conditions can help you adjust your hunting tactics and gear to the turkeys and setting, thus making you a more successful turkey hunter.

CHAPTER 18
THE GRAND SPORT AND TURKEY HUNTERS

Turkey hunting is a sport like no other. Yes it is hunting, and it does resemble other hunting sports in some ways, but to me turkey hunting is in a class of its own. What else can you hunt in the spring when the woods are coming alive after a long winter at rest? This is not to suggest that turkey hunters are somehow superior to other hunters, but rather that turkey hunting is different, and so are real turkey hunters! Becoming a successful turkey hunter is really about what we in academia like to call "life-long learning." In short, the learning never ends!

I have learned much from my many years of turkey hunting, and I am a better hunter for it. Perhaps most important to my turkey hunting success has been the willingness and ability to learn from my mistakes, from other turkey hunters, and from whatever other resources I could lay my hands on.

A good turkey hunter does not make the same mistakes over and over, but instead he analyzes his mistakes and makes adjustments to avoid making them again. If you are a turkey hunter, you probably understand very well what I mean. If you are just getting started, you will come to understand it. A "smart" turkey hunter not only learns from his mistakes, he is willing to learn from other hunters. I am hard-headed and generally want to do things my way. I learned the hard way that sometimes that is just plain dumb. When a good turkey hunter shares with you some of his "secrets" of success, pay close attention to his advice. I have been blessed to learn from some excellent turkey hunters, like my buddies Tim and Emory. Tim, who is the best public land turkey hunter I know, has killed grand slams on hard hunted public land—a grand slam is when a hunter takes, preferably in a single season, a gobbler from each of the 4 major subspecies in the United States. When Tim offers me advice about turkey hunting, I listen. My buddy Emory, who I actually introduced to the sport of turkey hunting, is an excellent turkey hunter and prides himself on his calling, always trying to master a bit more of the turkey vocabulary or a different calling device. I have learned some good calling techniques from Emory, and he has turned me on to some good calls. While I did not know him personally, I learned a lot from a fellow redneck from Alabama named Ben Lee. In my early years of turkey hunting in Georgia, when I really started getting serious about it, I listened to Ben's audio tapes (before video technology was readily available), read his book, and listened to him speak at seminars. God rest his soul, that fat boy from Alabama knew turkeys and turkey hunting, probably as well or better as any man I ever heard of, read about, or met.

Friends Emory and Ed, and the author, on their first Texas hunt in 2002. The results of a good day's hunt in Rio country!

I have learned much from reading about turkeys and turkey hunting. While I enjoy turkey hunting stories, I particularly enjoy reading articles and books about turkey behavior, turkey habitat, and turkey management, because I want to become, not only a better turkey hunter, but a better custodian of the resource, our turkeys. Articles about turkey behavior, turkey habitat, and turkey management can be found in hunting magazines and in scholarly Wildlife Management Journals. Turkey Country, a magazine published by the National Wild Turkey Federation, is an excellent magazine for the above, and it covers hunting tactics and equipment as well. I have a great book entitled The Wild Turkey: Biology and Management, compiled and edited by James Dickson. It is full of scholarly articles (based on research) about wild turkey habitat, behavior, population trends, and management, and it is very educational. I have read turkey hunting books by the very eloquent Colonel Tom Kelly, the best of which in my view was his first one entitled The Tenth Legion. In that book Colonel Kelly describes not only turkeys and turkey hunting, but also turkey hunters, comparing them to the elite Tenth Legion of the Roman army. My favorite book of turkey hunting stories is one entitled The Old Pro Turkey Hunter, by Gene Nunnery. His stories are short and entertaining. Reading good books can make you a better turkey hunter. Beyond my own book—I hope you are reading this because you are finishing my book—the ones mentioned here are well worth reading.

While turkey hunting videos are entertaining, and they are great for helping one learn the language of turkeys, they typically show "ideal" situations and successful hunts. Not many people would buy turkey hunting videos if most of the hunts ended up with missed or boogered gobblers, or days afield without so much as a gobble. Hunting videos also show hunters doing things I would never do—like talking and moving around with a bird in view. Turkey hunting videos are most often shot on private land where turkeys are carefully managed, and hunting is tightly controlled. If I were filming and producing turkey hunting videos, I would do the same. I can tell you from experience, seldom hunted turkeys on private land are easier to fool than those on hard-hunted public land. I hunt public land turkeys as well, so I know! Success on public land, or the hard-hunted private land of hunting clubs, etc., can be elusive even for a good turkey hunter. Most turkey hunting videos are for entertainment rather than instruction. I like to watch them when I cannot hunt turkeys, like during the off season.

Becoming a successful turkey hunter entails knowing turkey behavior, the habitat, having and knowing how to use the proper equipment, woodsmanship, and more. My goal in writing this book was to help others become successful, or perhaps more successful, turkey hunters. I hope you found the book both educational and entertaining. If you are a newbie, looking to get started, the knowledge I shared in this book should help you get started, and it gives you a foundation to build on. If you are an experienced hunter, you may have learned something new, refreshed your memory about things long forgotten, reinforced your own beliefs, or decided that you know more than I do. It might just be so! I have learned much from others over the years, so if you wish to share some of your knowledge with me, or ask me a question, feel free to contact me using the contact information supplied on the cover of this book. I hope I am never too old to learn something new that can make me a better hunter.

I have shared what I know about hunting the majestic wild turkey gobbler in the spring. You will note that I neglected fall turkey hunting, and I did so for a reason. I so enjoy the gobbling, drumming, and strutting of gobblers in the springtime, that I won't shoot a gobbler in the fall and deprive myself or others of the opportunity to hunt him during the spring mating season. I have no problem with others hunting turkeys in the fall where legal. I know how to take fall turkeys, and I have done it, but I just don't care to do it anymore.

Turkey hunting is a privilege we have in this great country wherein we can own guns, own property, use public land, travel freely, associate with whom we please, and hunt. For the privilege of hunting, we have certain responsibilities. I strongly urge everyone to purchase the appropriate licenses and tags and obey all game laws. Hunting regulations, including bag limits, are to preserve and protect our wildlife resources and to promote safe hunting. Those unscrupulous few who ignore bag limits are stealing from us all. You must hunt safely to protect yourself and others because turkey hunting is dangerous—you are fully camouflaged and making turkey sounds. You must respect the property rights of others. Ask permission if you want to hunt someone's property, and if they say no, stay off of it. You must preserve and protect the beauty of our public lands and private property as well. Drive only where vehicles are allowed, refrain from littering, and follow all other regulations designed to protect valuable public resources. Do the same on private land you are fortunate enough to hunt. Finally, you should share the sport with others.

In sharing our sport with others, we should be ethical hunters. If someone beats you to your favorite hunting spot, and you don't own it, back off and go somewhere else. I have seen unethical hunters park right next to or behind another hunter's truck, then walk into the same area to hunt, showing little regard for the other hunter or for safety. That is not only unethical, it is unsafe. Introduce others to the sport. Few things can compare with the thrill of seeing a newbie, particularly a child, take his or her first turkey. I get more thrill from that now-a-days than I do from killing a gobbler myself. Many of my hunting buddies feel the same way.

Many turkey hunters are very secretive about their hunting spots. I am as well. There is nothing wrong with that, but there is something wrong with hoarding the sport. Even if I won't tell a fellow hunter exactly where I am hunting, I am more than willing to point fellow hunters to places where I know they can find turkeys. People have often done that for me, so why not pass it on? It is not all about any one of us; it is about our sport!

We all need to recruit hunters to the sport, particularly young hunters. The future of our sport is assured by numbers—the number of turkey hunters in particular. Numbers give us the political and economic power to protect our sport from anti-hunting groups and anti-gun zealots. Join the National Wild Turkey Federation and participate in its programs and events. The NWTF, with its many state and local chapters, is our primary advocate for the sport of turkey hunting. Join the NRA as well. The NRA is on the frontlines in the battle to protect our 2nd Amendment rights. Joining both will run you about $70 a year. It's worth the money!

You have a responsibility to the magnificent bird that you hunt. Practice with your weapon before you hunt. Know your gun, and know your limitations. Take only good percentage shots and make every effort to recover a wounded turkey. It is the least you can do for a bird that can fill your spring mornings with such excitement that you think your heart is going to pound out of your chest. After 46 years of hunting, that excitement has never diminished.

In closing, I would like to comment on the comradery among turkey hunters. My turkey hunting buddies and I share a special bond. Perhaps there is something about the man that makes him a turkey hunter, or there is something that turkey hunting contributes to making the man. Maybe Colonel Tom Kelly had it right when he compared serious turkey hunters to the elite Tenth Legion of the Roman army. Perhaps there is something about us that makes us different. Turkey hunting is a special sport for special people. God bless and good hunting!

CPSIA information can be obtained
at www.ICGtesting.com
233993LV00005B

9 780615 470726